THE POLYAMORY TOOLKIT

A guidebook for polyamorous relationships

By Dan and Dawn Williams

Disclaimer Notice: Not all names in this book are real. Where real names are used, permission was granted by named person.

DEDICATION

We'd like to dedicate this book to all our past and current polyamorous partners, as well as everyone we have met along the way that helped us conceptualize and clarify these tools. From different classes and workshops to casual comments in the hallway, the impact you've had on us has been of great value.

Table of Contents

By Dan and Dawn Williams

INTRODUCTION

WHO WROTE THIS BOOK?

This book is co-authored by two people, Dan and Dawn. As two individuals with our own opinions, we wrote this book in such a way as to keep our own voices. We have our own perceptions of how these tools have been used in our relationships and our lives. Further, one tool may have been more impactful for one of us than the other. As we continue throughout the book, you'll see sections sub-headed with a "Dan says" or "Dawn says", to represent who wrote each part. If you have listened to our podcast (Erotic Awakening) or seen us present on polyamory and other topics, you'll hopefully be able to 'hear our voice' in these writing - how we write is very similar to how we speak.

You'll get to know us throughout the pages of this book. If you have a chance to meet us via presenting or other occasions, we think you'll come with a feeling like you already know us.

WHO ARE DAN & DAWN?

Because this is a book of experience, it might help you to know a bit more about the people writing it. But don't worry; we won't spend too much time here, as you'll get to know more about your authors throughout the book. This book is about the tools to assist you on your polyamory journey, and these tools are often developed via the steps (and tumbles) we took as we moved from it being a concept to practice to a way of life. But let's not jump too far ahead; we have lots of chapters in this book to explore the journey, but firstly, let's meet Dan and Dawn.

Dan says...

I come from two failed monogamous marriages. Some people don't like it when I said they are failed marriages, suggesting I must have learned something or at least had an occasional enjoyable moment, and although this is true, I look back and over all think 'Well, that sucked'. I got married for poor reasons, I tried to be the kind of partner I thought I was supposed to be and was generally unhappy and made people around me unhappy. The trick was I thought that I was supposed to put away who I was and become Husband Dan, just as the images of other husbands I see on TV and around me, at work and in social situations.

At first, it seemed great, but in a short time, it quickly became something that just didn't feel like me, like I was playing a role.

At the point that Dawn and I started our relationship, I knew one key thing that would need to be different – I would not give up who I am just because I am in love with someone. Our foundation would be built on mutual love, respect, compassion, but also around being ourselves. So, being me, whatever the authentic me is, and any relationship I am in would have to allow me to pursue that 'me'.

There are many labels I could mention here to help you get to know me. Labels like Buddhist, an amateur auctioneer, event producer, corporate America IT drone, author, presenter, podcaster, and in general someone who tries to be a fairly nice guy. As mentioned, since this book is based on our experience, you'll get to know me on the way (and hear some other labels that are part of the 'poly &...' aspect of me). But the other part of my makeup worth mentioning at this point is I used to have a pretty significant issue with drugs in my youth, up to my mid-twenties. Although that was a long time ago, it shaped one part of me that still exists as a foundation of who I am and how I live. There was a point in those years that I had no redeeming qualities and had I died (which is a bit amazing that I did not) it would have been an overall benefit to society. I didn't die, I got my shit together, and that left me with this – a deep gratitude in simply being alive and a sense that I need to be doing some small thing to be of value to the world (or at least my local community or peers). Otherwise, I am wasting a second chance.

Dawn says...

I had a previous marriage of 14 years. Pretty much what I took away from that marriage was what I didn't want the next time around, if there was a next time around. It wasn't all bad times, but I needed more. I needed something else. Once I found out that open-marriage was a real thing, and kink was a real thing, and I was totally interested in both, I just couldn't stay in a marriage that didn't allow me to explore either, without a LOT of guilt and shaming involved.

My story may sound familiar. I got married because I had to. Not because I was pregnant, but because as soon as I turned 18 and could leave home, I did. The guy I was dating at the time decided to rescue me and we rented a place together, which threw our grandparents into a tizzy. So, between trying to please them and the fact that our friends were getting married around the same time, we figured "what the hell" and followed suit. Not a good reason to get married I must say, but where I'm from, that story happened many times over.

This husband really wanted a wife that would take care of him, be there totally for him and just him. I tried to fit in that mold. I really tried. But all I did was make everyone around me unhappy as I became more and more unhappy myself. There were things I wanted to try, things I wanted to explore. But, when I mentioned it to my husband, he thought I was trying to .... Well, I'm not sure what he thought. He did not like the idea though.

You see, I believed myself to be polyamorous, though I didn't have a word for it. All I knew is that I didn't want to be denied the experience of intimacy with others just because I was married. I had only had sex with one other person consensually and I just couldn't imagine that I'd never have a chance to experiment with others or love others, or flirt with others, ever, because I was married. Hell, I'd never learned how to flirt. I had the same boyfriend for 2 years in high school and then I married the guy that was able to get me out of my parents' house.

I tried to be what he needed. I hid the fact that I was unhappy, as well as I could. But then the internet came along, and I realized that there was another world out there that I needed to explore. I was so excited; swinging, kink, open relationships, paganism, and so much more! I tried to pull the husband along with me. Tried to convince him it was going to be fun and we'd be ok. It didn't work. He lost another job, started drinking...we were done.

Then, mine and Dan's friendship started to change. We'd been friends since high school, but we'd never shared any deep secrets with each other or thought of dating each other, or anything along those lines. Until one day, it just happened. One night, the stars lined up and I took the risk and shared with him the horror of my past. Unfortunately, I come with a LOT of baggage; childhood abuse that I won't go into detail about, as this isn't the time nor the place. I had tried to share it with my husband (now ex), and he wouldn't let me. I understood why; he didn't want to hear how mean and selfish people could be. But that meant I had this secret that was eating me up. Then, one day I shared it with Dan. He listened. He heard. He didn't judge. He used skills he had learned in his 12 step meetings and rehab; from many years ago. And because he listened to me and didn't judge me, I began a relationship with someone whom I could trust with not only my secrets but my fantasies, as well.

One day I decided to share with him my thoughts about love and relationships and how I didn't think people should be tied down to just one person, and if they had a partner, that partner should be supportive of them. I also shared with him my kinky thoughts and was once again met with acceptance. So, we decided to move forward as more than just "friends".

I was in heaven. We were going to create our fantasy relationship, and everything was going to be great, utopia, or so I thought. If you have love, then everything will be perfect, right? That was my thought. Unfortunately, that is NOT what happened. Instead, all that baggage that I had shoved down for so many years, raised its ugly head and now if I wanted to move forward, I was going to have to do some heavy work with my memories, my low self-esteem, my fear of rejection, my fear of losing my new partner/friend and other character flaws. We were going to have to build a way to communicate and a way to support each other through these tough times. And so, we began to build tools so that we could move forward in a healthy way and be able to support each other's authentic self.

During the struggles, we didn't give up. OK, we came close a couple of times, but stuck with it knowing it was worth the effort. During these stuggles, if a tool that worked before didn't work the next time around, we created a new one. They were so positive for us that we started sharing them at weekend conferences. As we came up with more, we'd add them to the class, until they couldn't all be shared in an hour and a half. So, we created intensives, and now we'd like to share them with everyone!

I used to be a shy, introverted, people pleaser with low self-esteem and a strong dose of unworthiness, that had major issues with jealousy. Now, I'm a strong, confident, loving, powerful woman who embraces her authentic self. A woman that loves more passionately than ever before. Though, still an introvert, I'm also a mom of 2 great boys (not kids anymore), a grandmother, a Pagan Priestess, licensed clergy, an author, an event producer, a co-host of a popular podcast, a pet owner, a presenter and so much more!

WHY WE WROTE THIS BOOK

Dan says...

The background of how this book came to be is directly related to a very disappointing class we attended about a decade ago on jealousy. Although we had been practicing polyamory for a while at that point, we still struggled with feelings of jealousy and hoped we would find some tools on how to deal with it. Instead, the class was about how much jealousy sucked. It offered some psychological reasons on why it sucked and some historical context on jealousy sucking throughout the ages. But what it did not cover was simply what to do with the feeling! Were we broken because we felt it? Were we not 'true polyamory' people, because we had trouble dealing with the conflicting emotions of someone we loved wanting someone else? The presenter in the class simply came back to her main theme (how much it sucked) and we left the class feeling the same emotional turmoil we came in with.

This led us to dig in and start to develop our 'polyamory tool kit'. Through a lot of trial and error, we started to figure out what helps and what hinders in our poly processing. And although we read some great books and took more classes, for us, the most valuable things we learned came from experiences. The good, the bad, and the 'man I should have seen that train coming before it ran me over'. Some relationships we have had ended up great, others poor; some kept going as we all learned together. Relationships that led us from tears, to screams, to hugs, to make-up sex; each situation added to the polyamory toolbox as a 'what to do' or 'don't ever do'.

Remembering that class on jealousy from years before, Dawn and I started to develop a couple of classes on polyamory, focusing on action and tools. As we continued to present these classes, we got some great ideas from class participants as well as developed some new methods. Recently, someone told us - in this case, the Dan and Dawn and Karen "us" - we were an inspiration to them; that long-term successful polyamory could work. They pointed out that twelve years ago when Dan started dating Karen the last thing they expected was for us all to have bought a

12

house together. Yet, here we are, and between us we have all managed to maintain not only a relationship with each other, but other long-term loving relationships. At some point, people say "You should write a book!" often enough we think that maybe we should. And here we are.

So, this is the book! We will start quickly covering some terminology (just to make sure we have some common understanding and frame of reference) as well as take a look at what polyamory actually is versus other styles of open relationships. From there, we get started on tools, stories, and experiences. We will talk about how to build a foundation, what to do when you are feeling jealous (or anything else), first dates, ending relationships, living together, and lots more.

This book will also talk to you about sex. You will often hear that polyamory isn't all about sex and that is true. But sex does come up, and it can range from a nice side effect to a fantastic benefit to a huge issue to be considered. Some people say it can be the best - and the hardest - part of expanded relationships. We will share about navigating sex, sex with multiple polyamorous partners, and even address some polyamory specific sex tips for those who are curious or just voyeurs.

We have also had a few polyamorous relationships where sex wasn't part of it at all, and we'll talk about that as well. Yes, they do happen, and they are just as significant as the other relationships in our life.

What about polyamory and? You'll find that often polyamory gets mixed in with other subcultures and groups. Polyamory and geeky, polyamory and kink, polyamory and Leather and M/s and gamers and religion and a few others. You'll see some of that here as well as we share some tips on navigating the 'polyamory and?' waters. We've had some great - and not so great - experiences as we've walked in those mixed worlds.

Finally, this is a book that believes that love is infinite, polyamory can be a source of great joy and exponentially expanding experiences, and that you can be the designer of your own relationships. But it doesn't come without you actually doing it. This is not just a book of philosophies or theories. It is very much about the happiness and balance you can have if you are willing to put in the energy and effort. It is a book of tools you can apply. You can think of this book as a boat and a guide on how to row, and then it will be up to you to bend your back and start pulling. And that is ok. At first, you might have to get through some rough waters. Waters that seem beyond your measure to navigate perhaps. You'll be ok though. With each stroke, it gets easier, until your crossing is a relaxing day on a calm lake. We've been through some really rough seas, but it is immensely worth it.

Dawn says...

Rough seas... it's possible that we'll see some more rough seas. Whether it's with existing relationships or new relationships, only time will tell.

When we talk about our poly pod in workshops, we always talk about 'the stranger' - the person we haven't met yet, that could end up being a partner. Because we are not a closed poly pod and each of us date others and will continue to date new people, or at least that's the plan, 'the stranger' is always a possibility and with each new person is the possibility of someone going through jealousy again. Jealousy is not something that you fix once, and it doesn't appear again, for most of us. Who knows what might trigger it?

And when it happens, we look in our toolkit and pull out a tool that has worked before. If that tool doesn't work, we move to the next one. We may even find that it is going to take a special tool that we haven't needed before. If that's the case, it's time to develop another tool. It's not like we sat down one day and created the whole toolkit. The tools were developed one at a time as they were needed. And sometimes it took a while for a new tool to appear, as we didn't necessarily just pull one out of thin air. Sometimes we figured them out by accident because of something we heard, a dream or a random thought.... the proverbial 'aha' moments. So, I'm sure there are still some waiting to be discovered as we walk this journey.

In the meantime, we are here to share with you what has worked for us; the tools that we've developed over the last 20 years or so, starting with 'Porch time' - I'm pretty sure that was our first tool - right up to 'Perspective From other person's shoes', which I believe is the most recent.

These tools have been so valuable to our relationships and to each of us individually, that we took them on the road and have been sharing them over the years at kink, Leather and Sacred Sexuality events. We also talk about them on our podcast, Erotic Awakening. Now we'd like to make them available to everyone by writing this book.

WHO IS THIS BOOK FOR?

Dan says...

You might see that this book is written by two people who have been in a relationship for closing on twenty years and wonder if it is specifically intended for couples looking to add to a relationship. This is not at all the case; Dawn and I have maintained our relationship and we have also maintained many other romantic relationships. We have had intimate relationships (as well as simply dated) other people as individuals, and also as a couple. And we have dated couples as a couple as well.

Because Dawn and I have been together for a long time, on occasion we have been asked about couples' privilege - from, do we worry about it, do we take steps to prevent it from being an issue, etc. Couples privilege is a concept that suggests that an existing couple has an advantage over anyone else they are in a relationship with, and some people have been hurt by it, after the relationship started, being told their feelings or needs were not as important as those in the existing couple. This can be pretty painful to the new person and why couples bringing in a third gets a bad name. On the other hand, people have different reasons for entering a relationship with an established couple. Many do not want a fair share of the mortgage, kid raising, or other aspects. The concept of couples' privilege is more complex than the brief overview I just shared (a web search will allow you to find many arguments and a lot of debating on it if you like).

Anyway! This is not a book that is for or against couples' privilege nor is it written from a couples' privilege basis. But it is written by two people who have been together close to twenty years and who do many things as a pair; including writing books. Each of us has our own views, beliefs, and experiences. And we are partners and friends. When I have challenges with a girlfriend or want to share joys about a new relationship, Dawn is there to listen and give me a hug or a high five as called for. I don't see that as couples' privilege, it is an expression of our dance and the love we share.

Dawn says...

This style of writing books is the best for us, as we do have some different viewpoints and experiences. So, instead of trying to blend it together or try to write it with an outside view, we kept the view internal and spoke for ourselves.

Many of our examples will involve each other, because, well, we've been together for almost 20 years, and though we could have used more examples that involved other partners, the actual examples that were part of the 'aha' moments, usually involved each other.

These tools are based on our experience and come from a variety of places – 'Breaking Habitual Patterns' is something we learned in Dan's Buddhist practice and when we taught it in Canada, a psychologist that was in our audience pulled us aside and let us know that he also uses that with his clients, 'A Working Journal' is something I learned how to do in my spiritual studies, though it's called something else there and is about documenting attempts at manifestation.

So, though some of these tools are modified from other tools we may have learned somewhere else, none of them are theory. They are all based on our experience and some of them were intuitively made up, like 'The Joy Journal'.

Another thing that we've heard from in our workshops and presentations is that this information can be used by anyone in a relationship. We've had monogamous people in our classes before that either came in because they were curious or followed a poly partner in, or because there wasn't another class on the schedule that drew their interest and later told us that they are taking the tools home to use in their relationship, because the tools are just good relationship tools in general. Basically, this book can be used by anyone: new to poly, poly mature, or anyone wanting tools for working in any kind or relationship.

SPEAKING THE SAME LANGUAGE

Dan says...

There is a classic polyamory quote that goes "Polyamory is wrong! It's either multiamory or polyphilia, but mixing Greek and Latin roots? Wrong!"

This brief chapter is to talk about words and definitions. After all, many of the words we are going to use are common in poly circles, but you, the reader, may not be familiar with them. So, let's start with a few common ones you'll encounter in this book and define this "polyamory" thing.

Monogamy - This is the classic "one person with one other person", in a committed relationship, with no other romantic or intimate (or sexual) relationships. Most people appear to find this concept as the ideal, or at least it would seem according to popular media and culture. I could argue that with all the divorce and cheating that maybe it isn't as popular as people would guess but let's not digress.

Non-Monogamy - If you are not following monogamy, then welcome to non-monogamy, a huge umbrella that includes not only polyamory, but casual hookups, swinging, group marriages, and even cheating. If you are having romantic or sexual relationships with more than one person, then you are experiencing non-monogamy. So, does that put cheating and polyamory in the same boat? Not at all - read on...

Ethical Non-Monogamy - Although we have only added one word to the already defined non-monogamy, the difference by adding that word is rather huge. Ethical non-monogamy requires both honesty and consent. Thus, swinging, when everyone involved is aware of each other and not being sneaky about it, is ethical non-monogamy. But cheating is not. If you have two partners or twelve, and they are aware of each other and consent to the relationships, then it is a form of ethical non-monogamy.

Polyamory - Polyamory is a form of ethical non-monogamy. But where it is different than other forms of ethical non-monogamy is that it includes, as the Beatles would say, "Love, love, love". Simply put, polyamory is the belief that you can be romantically involved with more than one person. And you can do it in a way that those involved are aware of each other and consent to those relationships, and that those relationships can be healthy and enjoyable. Some people like to define this down to 'many loves', but that is a bit bare-bone for me. But that is just me - decide what makes sense for you.

Compersion - This is the state of feeling joy at your partner's joy. Buddhists call this mudita, which is defined as "a pure joy unadulterated by self-interest". You'll read lots more about compersion throughout this book, including how to cultivate it. For now, pretend your partner has just come back from a date and they have that sly smile that says that it went very well, and you feel good for them simply because they feel good. That is compersion.

Significant Other - Karen has been in my life for over ten years; we take vacations together, share a house together, and have, along with Dawn, a pet dog, and two cats. Karen is not my wife, as per the legal definition. But she is far more than a 'girlfriend'. Thus, the term significant other. It reflects anyone in your life that is more than a boyfriend/girlfriend to you but that isn't attached via another term like spouse or husband.

Metamours – Partners of my partners. For example, my partner Kat is married to a man named Nate. Thus, Nate is my metamour (or Meta). The level of involvement you have with metaphors may range from 'not at all' to 'big poly group movie nights every Thursday'. Different styles work for different people.

I'll note briefly that if you'd like to start an internet argument on a polyamory forum, these definitions would be a great place to start. Some people hate the word compersion; others find the term 'polyamory lifestyle' distasteful; others view the term 'poly' as an insult to Polynesian people. If you find words you prefer, and can still communicate, great! This is a book that focuses on the living and tools part of polyamory and thus we have no opinion on if a word is 'bad' or 'good', instead will ask 'is it useful to you?''. Plus, we suck at internet debating so will leave it to others who have time and energy for it.

Dawn says...

These are just some basic words from the world of Polyamory. There are many more. We don't expect everyone to agree with them, but it's how we use the words and how we are defining them for the book so that everyone is on the same page.

Through the tools and other writings, we'll also be using some other words that you may not be familiar with, but we feel we do a good job of explaining them in the writings themselves, so didn't add them to this list. And, during the writings, if we are pretty sure we know where the word came from, we tried to mention that as well.

TOOLS

Dan says...

One of the first polyamory classes Dawn and I taught was called "8 Poly Tools" and it was just that, eight of the polyamory tools we developed that helped us through interesting polyamory times. As time passed and new relationships came (and sometimes went) we developed more tools and at the point "8 Poly Tools" actually had over a dozen tools, we created a second class simply called "8 More Poly Tools". Between new relationships and feedback from other people, the number of tools expanded and in the following section, you'll find twenty-five tools.

Each tool includes reflections on the experience around when that tool was developed. You'll see a bit of background on the situation and how that tool was created and used. Moreover, you'll see it from both of our perspectives. For me, And Not Or was mind-blowing. For Dawn, she uses Compersion Journals more than me. We realize that not every hammer fits every hand. We want you to find the one that best fits yours.

TOOL #1 – DEVELOPING YOUR WHY

Dan says...

I can certainly recall more than once shaking my head and wondering "Why am I even bothering with this poly thing!?" The first time Dawn went on a date with another person (or slept with that person); or when a miscommunication left me reading a Facebook update that one of my partners is out with someone and I was left feeling betrayed; or when I walked into a room and see someone I am in love with kissing someone else, knowing they were there and on a date and nothing 'fishy' was going on... but my heart wasn't really ready to see it. I don't know about any other poly person, but more than once I thought 'can't I just be like everyone else and be turned on by just one human ever'?

Maybe you have faced a similar situation, and that has led you to pick up a book on polyamory. Or it might be a different reason - perhaps you are a single person who just met someone who said, 'by the way, I am polyamorous, would you like to meet my boyfriends?' Or maybe you are part of a couple that has decided to explore multiple loving relationships. It could be you are facing the tricky situation where you are part of a couple and one of you wants to start dating outside your existing relationship. Or perhaps you are in a situation where you are part of a growing triad that is facing some challenges, and it may be you are a polyamory veteran just looking for a new perspective. Polyamory can be pretty challenging.

If any of the above resonates with you - that moment of self-doubt where you wonder if polyamory is for you - then you'll find it useful to develop something we call "The Why".

The Why is an exercise in self-examination that answers the question, clearly and without reservation, of 'why did I decide to practice polyamory?'. This isn't the high-level question of nature or nurture. But instead, this is an understanding of your personal "Why". And it is something you can return to again and again when things get chaotic and you start down the path of self-doubt. Even when the question changes - from 'why did I think my beloved going out with someone else was a good idea' or 'why do I have to be home alone tonight' to the frustrated 'why do I have to put up with this bullshit!', you'll be able to rely on the answer of "The Why".

Because if you can get here, get deep enough to touch the heart of why you are exploring polyamory when you were (probably) raised to think monogamy was not only normal but the only possibility, then you'll be able to establish an eye of the storm that you can rest on as you struggle with those different questions (and emotions and situations that brought those questions on).

So! How do you develop your personal 'Why'? Well, the good news is, you already have - or at least have started. For some reason, you are here now, reading this book. How come? What lead you to want to love in a different way?

For me, the Why started with the question 'why have all my previous relationships ended up the same, with me feeling either unhappy (at the minimum) or me acting outside of my desired ethical boundaries' (which is a fancy way of saying I started to search for a new relationship prior to ending the one I was in). As I began the relationship with Dawn, I wanted to make sure that I was not going to repeat the mistakes I've made so far and that I was addressing the core of what I wanted, needed, and expected in a relationship. So, I looked at myself and realized that I am not really a monogamous person. I can't say I thought of it in that way exactly - and had not yet heard the word polyamory. But I recognized enough that I could express to Dawn that we would not be exclusive to just each other and - my reality is that I could love more than one person, that I am attracted to lots of people, and sometimes I want to act on that attraction, and that these characteristics - and this was a huge thing for me - didn't need to be 'fixed'. I was not broken, I just didn't follow the norms that most people seemed to have. What I needed to be was accepted by Dawn, as well as other future partners, and by myself. This leads me toward a path of understanding ethical non-monogamy. And that I was not alone in this view.

It took some time before the words and understanding really came to me, but for me, the first part of the Why is 'I am a polyamorous person'. And it is more than just the words 'I am polyamorous'. It is the understanding, the looking in the mirror and seeing that which is true, the realization that it is as much a core aspect to who I am as 'I am an introvert' or 'I have a sense of humor'.

So, part 1 is that core understanding of who I am.

The next part of my 'Why' is that I realize that I want other people around me to be happy. That I really do believe that sharing joy and love is a sign of love, and that there is no reason for me to feel a need to horde love or attention. It does not serve those I love, it does not serve me. It doesn't feel like who I am or who I want to be. The vision I have for myself - the who I want to be - is someone who isn't afraid of love or my partners love; I don't want to be selfish or motivated by greed (if you love him, you won't have enough for me). And I don't want my partners to be treated like objects that I am afraid of losing, thus I hang on too tight. So, the second part of the Why for me is the realization that I wanted to be, at my core, generous and joyful in my partner's self-actualization, even when that meant more than I could provide.

The last part in this foundation of my own personal Why is I want to my partners to support me in whatever I do. And that very much includes who I do (who I love, who I make love to, who I tie up and tickle, who I make googly eyes at), and since I expect that from my partners, they should be able to expect that from me. So, this too became part of my foundation, the 'we all want the freedom to be ourselves, whatever direction that takes, and if I ask it of you, I will give you the same'.

Successfully dealing with all the emotional aspects of beginning a life that includes polyamory often means a continuing self-discovery journey. But the Why is my baseline; that personal mission statement, that recognition of who you are and who you want to be.

How you find your Why is your journey. This book is full of tools that will help you get there. As you read, keep a notepad nearby, title it My Why and keep track of those things that are true for you, and at some point, if someone says, "Why are you putting up with that polyamory thing?" you'll be able to smile and know you have an answer.

Dawn says...

I never really thought of this as a tool, but the more I think about it, the more I believe this is the first tool that should be used.

If polyamory is such a struggle, why are you putting up with it? Funny, no one really asks people, 'if monogamy is such a struggle, why are you putting up with it?'. When I was in a monogamous relationship and it was such a struggle and I was having tingly feelings for other people and I didn't like being tied down to one person, no one suggested that maybe monogamy wasn't for me. No one gave me tools. Basically, when I told my mother and my mother-in-law that I wasn't happy, they told me that they weren't either, but they stuck it out because that's what you do. I didn't want to 'stick it out'.

So, why do I put up with all the work that has been involved in becoming a mostly successful polyamorous person and partner? Because I'm polyamorous. It's that simple.

I've dated more people since being married to Dan, then I had my whole previous life. OK, to be honest, I had dated more people in the first 2 years of being married to Dan than in my whole previous life, and it was amazing!!! We may talk a lot about jealousy and rough times and having to learn tools to make this work, but think, we learned these over 20 years! There have been many good times in between that aren't discussed so much in a tool book.

I had some AMAZING experiences, experiences that I had only fantasized about before, over the last 2 decades, and I plan on having more amazing experiences over the next 2 decades if not longer. The Universe has brought some amazing, fun, deep, beautiful people into my life and it's made the work all worth it.

TOOL #2 – AND NOT OR

Dan says...

My significant other met someone new. That is fine – we are polyamorous, and it certainly isn't unexpected that new people pop up in our lives, but what sometimes throws me for a loop is that the someone they met is so very...well, not me. By that, I mean that sometimes my partners end up with a person in their life that is more this, less that, better at, not concerned about, happy to share this, enjoys that thing I hate. And the more pronounced the difference, the more a worm of doubt generates in my head, saying 'if my partner likes (that), then do they still want me?'.

Most recently, Karen met a "not me" and they enjoy country music and motorcycles, two things I had no clue she even liked. Since I don't like (country music, with a few exceptions) and something I've thought about doing but never have (getting a motorcycle), it never occurred to me that Karen might. But with the new person, she and the new guy have gone to a variety of country concerts; and she tells me that riding on the back of his Harley is like having a mobile vibrator (she likes a lot of other things about riding his motorcycle, but this is the one that struck me the most).

So how do I wrap my head around the fact that she likes these new (different) things? And does it mean she doesn't like the old things...you know...me?

The tool I keep in mind here is 'And, Not Or'. This is a reminder that polyamory isn't about her picking him over me, or her liking a type of music and suddenly hating all others. Polyamory is an abundance way of living. We get to have our cake and eat it too. She gets to enjoy having motorcycle time and country hits with him AND enjoy a nice walk listening to chill techno with me.

Another example of why this is so great is because I don't drink. But Dawn wants to experience doing a wine tour with someone that actually knows what they are talking about. So, she can go with her boyfriend and enjoy different wines (who knew Ohio had wine country?) AND she gets to enjoy coffee shops and board games with me.

'And, Not Or' is a great reminder to me that I am still important, the things we do are still fun/enjoyable for her, and that just because she has something new doesn't mean it is 'out with the old'.

Dawn says...

This was a great tool for me to learn. I had a really hard time in the beginning. Well not at the beginning, but near the middle of our time being poly. That's because, at the beginning we were co-amorous, which means we dated other people together. I'm bi, Dan isn't. So, it was usually another woman or a couple that we would date together. There wasn't much to be jealous over or to worry about when we were dating someone together.

Then, over time, we decided to branch out. It had been hard to find people that matched both of us, so we decided to do things on our own. It was rough for me. Every time he brought in a new potential partner, I'd look at the differences. Why would he want to spend time with her? I thought we (Dan and I) were a perfect match? As a matter of fact, I'm not far off. We are about a 95% match. For me, I don't date others to fill in a hole or because I'm not getting a need met. I'm dating others because I have the capacity to love more than one person at a time and enjoy seeing life through my experiences with various people.

But even though I know this about me, it's hard to remember that about my partner. That he (Dan) or any of my partners, aren't dating others because there is something lacking in me. When you have low self-esteem though, it's really hard to keep that in mind, and even though I was in an amazing relationship that we designed together, I still had low self-esteem hidden deep. So, anytime he found someone else, I'd look for the differences, OR worse, I'd even look for some of the similarities. If I found differences, it meant that I was missing something. If I found similarities, it was because what he likes about me, I didn't have enough of or wasn't good enough. So, my emotions told me. Ouch.

Funny, how we convince ourselves of these things.

We'd talk and talk about this....and by talk...some of you can picture what these talks looked like. During them, he'd assure me that this was not the case. At this time, we didn't have the language to really put this into a way that I could understand though. It was years before Dan popped up with the phrase 'and not or'.

That's when it all clicked. He wasn't taking someone on a car trip because he didn't like traveling with me. That person wasn't going to replace my road trip time with him. It wasn't an 'or'. Instead, he got to experience a trip with someone else. It was about it being a different experience. It was an 'and'.

If my boyfriend dates someone new, it's not because he's replacing me. It's because we are poly and dating others is what we do. We've discussed this and it's in our agreements. He will date others. AND date me. We can date multiple people. It's an 'and'.

Though it really clicked for me when I started developing my own 'other' relationship, that even though I'm dating others, it's not because I have an interest

26

in replacing anyone else in my life. I can have a romantic relationship with Dan, and the boyfriend, and the girlfriend, and others. I can have as many 'Ands' as I can handle.

Hearing this concept, was like taking a deep, clear breath. Ahhhhh. Things clicked in ways they hadn't clicked before.

TOOL #3 – EXPERIENCE
IT DIFFERENTLY

Dan says...

The first time that Karen went to visit her new boyfriend in Pittsburgh, I thought "Well, I guess we will never go to Pittsburgh - she has 'done that, been there' ". The same thought struck me when Dawn would go to a restaurant with a partner or visit a coffee shop. My thinking was 'it is their thing now/no longer something to be done with me'

For me, this same type of thinking can come up when a partner has sex with someone else for the first time; and even more so when it is something they don't do with me (a specific kind of play or sex that I don't enjoy). I think that since they are doing something with the new partner now, they won't be interested in sex with me – same old boring me.

This kind of thinking can escalate into a feeling of scarcity, for example, a commercial for a new restaurant comes on and partners want to claim "Mine!" so they can be the one that experiences it with you.

The reality is that anything I do with Dawn is a different experience than I have even if I do the same thing with Kat or Karen or whoever else. What do I mean by this? I look at things this way, there is this entity called Dan, and then there is a Dawn as well. But when Dan & Dawn do something together, then it is this third entity that is Us (a combined experience of Dan & Dawn). Now you don't have to think esoterically about this "Us entity", but it is my experience when I go to a movie with Dawn, we have a pattern we follow - Dawn sits on my right, doesn't stop at the concession stand, knows when to stop talking, and holds my hand and enjoys the movie. But when Karen goes to a movie with me, she sits on my left, always stops and gets candy and water, and had the occasional comment during the movie. Neither of these is 'good' or 'bad', but they give me a different experience. And this extends to going to concerts, restaurants, dancing, and sexy time as well. The way Dawn and I (do sex) and the way that I am with anyone else is both the same (tab A goes in slot B) but it is vastly different as well, and that is how it should be - again, not 'better' or 'worse', but different. Sometimes you want Pad Thai and sometimes you want Waffles, both of them are yummy but different.

Dawn says...

I can clearly remember driving to Toronto through Niagara Falls and being on the phone with my sister. She asked what we were doing, and I told her we were going to a camping event in Toronto to teach some classes on polyamory and power exchange. 'Oh, then are you going to stop at Niagara Falls?'. I told her no because he and Karen had just been there last week. Here reply was 'so?', as I watched Dan take the exit for Niagara Falls on the Canadian side. I looked at him with a question and he shrugged his shoulders. I replied to my sister, 'well looks like we are stopping at Niagara Falls.'

I hung up the phone with my sister and asked him why we were going to Niagara Falls? We hadn't talked about making this stop. He asked me if I liked Niagara Falls. I told him I loved it there the couple of times we had been in the past. 'Well, why didn't you ask if we could stop?', he asked me. 'Because you were just there with Karen last weekend, why would you want to stop again?'

He was confused. Sometimes he is a little more poly enlightened than I am. His reply was, 'it's a whole different experience with you. Why wouldn't I want to go?" Which didn't mean it was better or worse, just different.

Ok, that makes sense, I guess. But, it's really true and it took me starting my own loving relationship with my boyfriend, Raymond, to figure this out. Just because I do something with Dan doesn't mean I don't want to do so with Raymond, and just because I do something with Raymond doesn't mean I don't want to do it with Dan, or anyone else. It's different, so go into it with the attitude of 'enjoy it differently'. It's not going to be the same as with the other person. The energy you create together, with different backgrounds and different experiences and different likes/dislikes, is going to create a different experience. Enjoy it!

TOOL #4 – BREAKING HABITUAL PATTERNS

Dan says...

We mention a few times in this book that there are times when we have had a partner tell us something and we did not respond as our best self. One of the big ones for me was when I found out one partner had slept with someone new after she and I had been together at a party and although this was expected – they planned to spend the night together – I was out in the parking lot and, via the phone, screaming at them in a rage.

It wasn't until later that I looked at the situation and genuinely wondered – why did I react that way? I should not have been surprised. I get being upset or even angry, but in a rage?

It wasn't until later that I found out about habitual patterns and a way to escape them. I've explored them from both a psychological view (an aspect of cognitive behavioral therapy) but am much more comfortable explaining from the Buddhist perspective and the works of Ken McLeod or Pema Chödrön. It comes down to the same thing. But let me start at the beginning.

A habitual pattern is a mechanism of reacting to life. Sometimes they work, but more often than not, they don't serve us anymore, because they happen without thinking based on who we were, instead of who we are.

Have you ever found yourself screaming at a person who cut you off in traffic? Or making a biting remark to someone who shared some news? Or any course of action that you felt like you didn't have control of...and that you feel doesn't really reflect who you are. These may well be habitual patterns that are ingrained in you. From a polyamory perspective, I easily identify jealousy as a habitual pattern. Mentally there is no reason for me to be reacting with jealousy. I am polyamorous, I have many partners, and I like it that my partners have partners. Yet, I find out they have a new flame, and my initial reaction is a grumpy "oh great another new person". This is a pattern that I learned from monogamous days and it no longer serves me.

So, how do you reprogram them? First, understand that hear about new partner to screaming 'How could you do that to me!' has many steps between the two. Five steps to be precise. Let's look at them.

First is sensory stimuli. Perhaps that monk that lives in a cave can avoid sensory stimuli, but you and I likely never will. From the news of a new partner to being cut off in traffic to the smell of popcorn, we have tons of sensory stimuli happening all the time. Let's not worry about it. In this book we are going to assume you like having a phone and a car and popcorn and assume it stays as is.

Second is feeling tone. All this sensory stimuli first hits us as at a very basic level – is it pleasant, unpleasant, or neutral? For example, if I tell you I have a Yamaha motorcycle, then you will likely either respond with "Oh, those are awesome, I had a 650 V Star, they are great (pleasant)" or "Bah, only Harleys are real bikes (unpleasant)". Or with "Oh? (neutral)". Again, as this is neither a psychological or Buddhist text, we are going to just be aware of them. In the case of 'hear about new partner' is the sensory stimuli, the feeling tone in this scenario is 'unpleasant'

Third is interpretation, and this is where things get interesting. How does our previous experience, knowledge, image makers, media, and everything else that has helped shape us, interpret things on a very base level? When the sensory stimuli of 'hear about new partner' comes up, my habitual pattern is to interpret this with fear and selfishness. I've had many years of being told 'if she finds someone new, you are out!'. So, although I understand and believe in polyamory, my habitual pattern kicks in and I have a deep-seated process kick off that says Uh oh, someone new and better – they are leaving me!

So, 'hear about new partner' is the sensory stimuli, the feeling tone in this scenario is 'unpleasant', and interpretation is 'they are leaving me!'.

This leads us to our fourth part – emotional response. You probably know this one. It comes with a physical reaction as well: rapid heartbeat and shortness of breath, or lethargy. From fear to anger to jealousy to all those other reactions that make us – whether we like it or not – human beings – kick in. We will come back to this one in a moment, but first, let's recap. 'Hear about new partner' is the sensory stimuli, the feeling tone in this scenario is 'unpleasant', and interpretations is 'they are leaving me!', and now we have an emotional response – 'fear into anger'.

This leads to that fifth step – action. Also known as putting a fist through a wall, laying on your horn, hiding in a dark corner, or, in my case, screaming into a phone in a rage.

How does any of this help you not repeat those behaviors? Well, it really does start here – just knowing it is a pattern and it has certain steps. This is the first thing we need to know in choosing to respond the way we always have, or in developing a new way.

The key is we want to get to that third step, interpretation, and allow ourselves time to re-evaluate those sensory stimuli prior to it hitting emotional response or action.

We do that via a few different tools. Elsewhere in this book we mention meditation, and this really does have a very direct impact on our awareness and ability to slow down our habitual patterns.

Another tool to try is to take a daily inventory of our actions. Look at how we responded with as much neutrality as we recall. Remember this is about changing us, not anyone else, and if we find out that our actions have been outside of who we want to be and has impacted others, then apologize to those impacted. This helps us get to the point of not reacting - we train ourselves that if we keep doing what we are doing, we will soon have to apologize for it, and isn't it better to just change direction right now?

Dawn says...

Habitual patterns can be my nemesis. I react a certain way because I've always reacted a certain way. Well, some of those patterns are based on defense mechanisms or fears from the past and truly don't serve me now.

I want to react to life based on the present and from a place of abundance, not from past baggage, past people's actions and a sense of scarcity. Some of the tools I've learned over the years have helped with this, but there is a huge one that I learned from Dan and a book he was reading, and then again at a weekend Buddhist/meditation retreat I attended, and it made everything click.

As Dan stated above, there are 5 steps from the initial stimuli to the reaction, and though that time may be a snap of the fingers when it happens, there are steps in between the beginning and the end of these steps.

When we've taught this around the country, we have people stand up in front of the class, each of them holding a sign showing what their step is, and we show how to slow down the steps. Though, it's easier to slow down the mind with adding meditation to your daily routine, just seeing it visually like that shows you that you have a choice in how you react.

For one, start with your reaction. You feel the adrenaline, the fear (step 4), but you decide not to yell and scream or punch the wall. You decide not to hide under the covers or have that drink. You recognize this is part of the step of breaking a habitual pattern. I go jog on the treadmill instead, to break down the chemicals in my body that were stirred up. Otherwise, we end up suppressing and they come out later in passive aggressiveness. Or so I've experienced.

But you can't stop there, or you will always be working on not reacting to emotions that are the true habitual pattern. So, move on to the emotional response.

When you feel that habitual emotional reaction happen, breathe. Don't let it take ahold. Go into manual mode or into your mantra (covered in other sections of the book). Remind yourself that this emotion could be a habitual pattern and not really based in the truth of the moment. Now I'm not saying it's not a valid emotion, but you won't know if it's based on reality until you start peeling off the habitual patterns.

I can remember one day where I was feeling super jealous and unhappy. I got looking at it and then wondered, "am I jealous because something is truly wrong that needs to be fixed? Or am I jealous because I'm 'supposed' to be jealous because my husband is dating someone else?" I had been working on not having the reaction and was at the step of looking at my emotional reaction and this is what spoke to me.

I was raised in an environment where if a spouse even looked at another person of the opposite gender, there was hell to pay. Everything was about scarcity and fear and control, and though I didn't want to live my relationships that way, that's what was happening. Habits based on modeling.

So, once I realized that most of my reactions were based on this, I started looking at interpretation. Whoa. This is where a lot of work needs to be done. If I have low self-esteem going on that day.... which was normal back when I was working on my healing path.... I'd always interpret it as something negative - "Of course he wants to go out with someone else, look at who he's stuck with, high maintenance girl" or something along those lines. Again, this is where I'd use one of my other tools, usually 'Manual mode' or my 'mantra', to get beyond this and tap into the logic of the situation.

Honestly, my goal is to get to the 2nd step of the pattern, 'Feeling tone'. I want my baseline for reactions to stimuli to be neutral, a sense of equanimity. If I can get there, then I don't have to worry so much about interpretation, or emotional response or action. Simply because they will be based on a non-judgmental thought process instead of a habitual one.

I truly didn't understand equanimity when I first heard of it. What do you mean not having a strong emotional response? All of my responses are strong and emotional and based on judgements. They were absolutely tiring to me and everyone around me. Then, slowly as I did the work it started to fall into place. My emotions have been much more manageable. As a survivor, I don't do transitions or change very well. But with this understanding of habitual patterns and understanding that most of my reactions are based on fear and understanding that there is a point in these reactions where I can decide not to react the way I usually do, there is more balance when my world changes.

TOOL #5 – UNCOMFORTABLE VS WRONG

Dawn says...

I used to have, and sometimes still do, this emotion when one of my partners starts to date someone new or do something new with one of his current partners. Because I couldn't figure out what the emotion was, but it was usually a negative emotion, I would label it as 'wrong'.

By labeling it as 'wrong' though, that meant that I felt that what Dan was doing was wrong. That didn't feel right either. He wasn't doing anything wrong. We are polyamorous, this is what we do.

One day he asked me if I really thought what he was doing was wrong, or if I was just 'uncomfortable' with what he was doing. Huh! I looked at it. If I was labeling it wrong, and he wasn't doing anything wrong, maybe it was a different emotion. 'Uncomfortable'. I was definitely feeling uncomfortable, and just because something feels uncomfortable doesn't mean the other person is doing something wrong. Damn it. That meant it was my issue, not his, which means, I have more work to do.

I don't know if I was putting this in the box of 'wrong' because of how the emotion felt, or because there was a piece of me that felt this is what I'm supposed to be feeling. Emotions can be so confusing sometimes, and if my logic and emotions don't line up, it's even more confusing.

But, because Dan gave me another word to work with, I was able to really look at the emotion for what it really was. Well, 'uncomfortable' could mean a lot of different things, at least it wasn't 'wrong', and my partner didn't feel the need to go on the defensive, knowing he wasn't doing anything wrong.

Once I figured out that the emotion was 'uncomfortable', I was able to look at why it was uncomfortable. Whenever I thought it was wrong and would look at the logic behind it, I'd get lost and confused. When I reworded my emotion to 'uncomfortable' I was able to see more clearly.

Was I feeling funny when he started dating someone new? Yes. Was it wrong? No. So, now I could look at my emotions and figure it out. Why was I feeling uncomfortable? Low self-esteem? Fear? Jealous of the time lost? Feeling ignored? Feeling left out? Territorial? Whatever the answer, these are things we can work with.... things I can work with.

When we think the emotion is that they are doing something wrong, and that's not really what is going on, then we are working with the wrong ingredients to start with and the answer and resolution are going to be impossible to track down.

When Raymond is texting someone else, is that feeling 'uncomfortable' or 'wrong'? Let's say we think it is 'wrong'. Is it really? Unless rules have been set up around communication times and styles, shouldn't they be investing time in the new relationship? Wouldn't you want your new person to be texting you? So, it's not wrong...then what is it?

Remember, if something is 'wrong' then you are putting all these emotions on the person you believe is doing something wrong. Then it turns into the blame game and puts them on the defensive. If something is just 'uncomfortable' then you can look in the mirror and do the work that is needed to make the situation more comfortable. It could be asking for some rules to be put in place while you work on this, or better yet it could be figuring out what is making you feel uncomfortable and using your tools to help shift your emotions.

Flip the situation. If I'm going to the movies or out to a club with the boyfriend, am I doing anything wrong? I'm poly. I have more than one partner. I don't want my husband (or any partner) to feel like I'm doing something wrong. He knows where I'm at and he knows who I'm with. What I'm doing is perfectly within my boundaries/rights and agreements. So, am I doing anything wrong? No. But, he has a funny feeling that he doesn't know how to label. If he was to ask a monogamous friend what that feeling was, they would lean towards the fact that of course he feels this way because I'm out with someone else, therefore, I'm doing something wrong.

If he was to talk to a poly friend, they may give him other advice. Am I doing something wrong? No. So, instead, the feeling he is feeling is something else. We label it 'uncomfortable'. Now he gets to look at himself and see what is causing this feeling. Is he afraid I'll have more fun with the other person? Is he afraid that I'll leave him? Does he want me home with him instead so that we can play our video game together? Whatever it is, it is now his issue to deal with. He may ask for my help. I don't mind helping at all. But I don't want him to blame me if I'm truly not doing anything wrong, just like he doesn't want me to blame him.

Uncomfortable. Give the word a try. It is much more helpful than the blame game of 'wrong'.

Dan says...

This seems like such a minor adjustment, but it is a true gateway to getting beyond some of my difficulties. As Dawn said, when you do something that results in me feeling uncomfortable, then that leads to options to resolve that feeling. I can ask you not to do it - and that is ok sometimes by the way. Your partner may be within the boundaries you have set forth with coming over with a fresh hickey, but if it makes you more comfortable to have them text first, then why not be gracious and do so? For me, that was the exact situation I was in - not sure why hickeys turned my belly so much, but it did. Time went by and I realized I didn't care anymore.

TOOL #6 – COMPERSION JOURNAL

Dawn says...

About 8 years into our polyamory journey, I found myself really struggling. This is about the time that we switched from coamory to a form of polyamory that had us dating separately. The first form of polyamory that we tried, coamory, was really safe; we were doing it together, holding hands and jumping into the unknown together. So, there really wasn't a lot to stress about, not a lot of fear. I would have a couple of blips every now and then, but nothing like what happened when we started to date separately.

I got the idea for this tool after looking back on my journals and my old tapes. I was an avid journaler; something I had learned to do as a kid, to dump all my crappy feelings. Then, Dan bought me a mini-tape recorder so that I could 'journal' while driving to and from work. I used the little hand-held recorder a lot and I went through many notebooks, writing every spare moment, trying to figure out my feelings.

One day I came across some of the tapes while cleaning out my car and decided to listen to them. They were full of so much pain, anguish and fear; stories that my low self-esteem and fearful inner child was telling me. As I listened to the old tapes, literally, and re-read the journals - I started asking myself why I was putting myself through so much anguish.

Why was polyamory causing all these negative emotions? I'd known that I was polyamorous for many years, since before I had language for it. I was positive that I wanted to live that way. I believed in the idea that I had enough love for more than one person. Yet, here I was struggling with jealousy, struggling with not feeling good enough, struggling with feeling unworthy, struggling with feeling weak, struggling with fear. It was so painful, and then it felt shameful because after all these years I was still struggling. I felt I should be beyond all this.

37

One day, I was talking with someone about this struggle and that I couldn't believe I was still finding this so challenging. They asked me if I was noticing the dates on my journaling. Did I notice how much time there was between entries? Did I only write about the negative feelings or was I writing about the good stuff as well? Of course not. I had always journaled to get rid of the yucky stuff marching about in my head and heart.

I looked through my journals again and realized that it would be months between entries, months of feeling ok in my world, so I didn't have anything to process. Where were all those writings? Where was the joyful stuff? I had to have experienced good stuff, otherwise I wouldn't have made it for as many years as I had. I'm not an emotional masochist.

So, I decided to shift my attitude and focus on the positive stuff. If I had journals for all the bad stuff going through my head, why not a journal for all the good stuff? I bought a beautiful pink leather journal and promised myself that I'd only write down happy, joyous experiences with polyamory in this journal. It's my 'compersion journal' or my 'joy journal. Every time I experienced something that made me happy, I'd write about it. This process helped turn my focus from the negative and shift it to the positive. I would actually start looking for and paying attention to the joyful moments in our polyamory journey. It went a long way in changing my perception of what I was experiencing.

This tool caused a major turning point for me when I was really struggling with poly. But now when I have a rough moment, I have physical proof that happiness and joy have taken place during this journey.

The happy moments far outweigh the moments of struggle. I just needed to see it in writing to prove it to myself. Because of my past baggage, I had focused more on the struggles than the joy. It's human nature or at least it's my human nature. It's probably not everyone's nature, but when you grow up in an environment that is all about the struggle, it really takes a lot of work to realize that there are a lot more positive moments than I realized.

I still have this journal. I still write in it and it has some really amazing moments in it of love and compersion. Since the journal is a physical item, if I'm feeling down, I can actually pick it up and hold it and read it and remind myself of all the great experiences I've had over the years.

Dan says...

There are occasions where I will happily advise 'fake it till you make it', and the compersion journal can be a tool here as well.

When feeling low or down about a partner doing something that is poly - maybe your head knows it is fine and within any agreements you have, but your heart is having trouble - break out the compersion journal and write about being happy. Sure, it might feel like a work of fiction at first, but what I've found is if I start that process, it will make me examine what I am feeling, which starts me on the path of processing it, which more often than not leads me to actually feeling compersion! Sure, I might start off with a halfhearted "I guess I am sort of happy that Dawn has someone to go to a wine tasting with tonight..." to realizing that I don't actually like wine. I do like Dawn being happy, and once I get past the illusion of being abandoned, then it actually is kind of a win-win situation, and when I picture my partner experiencing new things, having fun, smiling, and release the feeling of things being done 'at me', then true happiness isn't far behind.

TOOL #7 - DON'T TAKE THINGS PERSONALLY

Dawn says...

Of course, I take things personally. Everything is about me, right? Well, not so much as it turns out. Other people's actions certainly 'feel' like I should be taking it personally. My emotions tell me it's personal, but it's really not - not usually anyway.

When one of my partners goes out with another partner and I feel jealous or lonely or fearful, sometimes I don't want to admit that I'm experiencing these feelings and am responsible for them. Instead, it's easier to put the blame on someone else and to think that they are 'doing' something to us or behaving a certain way because of something we did, and we are being punished for it. But usually, that has nothing to do with what they are doing.

Realizing that I was blaming my emotions on someone else's actions and not taking personal responsibility for them, had me looking for another tool. And as the Universe does, it provided me with a book that had a tool that has really helped me out. The book is, 'The Four Agreements'[1]. It has some great wisdom in it, but one of the things I took away from it that has really helped me in my poly experiences is the idea of 'Not Taking Things Personally'. Easy right? The world doesn't revolve around us, right? Well, this idea is harder than it sounds. For some reason, most of us think that other people's actions have something to do with us, because we see life through our own eyes, our own filters, our own perceptions, but most of the time, other people's actions really don't have anything to do with us.

When someone cuts me off in traffic, which is one of the easiest examples to use, it has nothing to do with me, but we take it personally, don't we? I know I do. They are out to get me, or they think they are better than me, or something, and we react as if it's a personal affront. We take it personally. But is that really true?

---

[1] Don Miguel Ruiz and Janet Mills, The Four Agreements: A Practical Guide to Personal Freedom (A Toltec Wisdom Book)

I can remember a car that sped past me in a gravel parking lot as I was pulling in, and it raced to the front of the parking lot, taking the last spot in the row. They got out of their car as I pulled up behind them. I got out and yelled at them (simply because they had scared me so bad). They looked at me in total surprise and said, 'why would you think this has anything to do with you? My kid is in the hospital, (pointing across the street) and I need to get to him." And they took off running.

That blew my mind. How egotistical of me to think it was about me. My thought had been, 'maybe I wasn't moving fast enough for them', 'maybe they needed to show me their car was better than mine', 'maybe they liked showing off', 'maybe they want to scare me', 'maybe they don't like my bumper stickers' or something along those lines. Instead, I find out that I'm not even in their thoughts. Huh.

To finish that story, I felt so bad for yelling at them and making myself part of their story, that I got a pen and paper from my car and left them an apology on their windshield. No need for my issues to add to their bad day, but it struck me, what other situations had I assumed someone else's focus was on me? How many other times had I taken things personally when I shouldn't have? How many times have I had negative, defensive reactions to something like my partner spending time with his other partner, or going on a trip with them, or whatever it is that they are doing? I need to remember that usually, it has nothing to do with me. As we talk about with another tool, this is 'and not or'. He (or she) enjoys being out with other people and experiencing life with others.

When a metamour wants to spend time with one of my partners, it has nothing to do with me. It's because they want to spend time with that partner. It's not to show me that he'd rather spend time with them than me, or anything like that. It really has nothing to do with me, for example, there was a time that Dan decided to spend the night with another partner instead of me. I got lost in the story of why he made that decision, and, in my story, I took it personally. My story that I told myself said that he didn't like spending time with me and would rather spend time with someone else. It totally had me in a downward spiral. I really believed that his decision was completely about me. If you think of it, that sounds a little narcissistic and selfish, doesn't it? And if I bring it up to him, 'why don't you like me anymore?' he will look at me in confusion, clueless about how I came to that conclusion.

What I learned and need to remember is that usually decisions aren't made like that. They aren't out to get you. Decisions are made based on someone's desires or needs or based on their own stories. They don't usually even know your story enough to know how to do things to you personally.

Remember that everyone is working from their own filters, their own baggage, and their own stories. You included.

Dan says...

Let's say you belch in the elevator. Happens, right? If you are alone, you probably don't even think about it. If other people are on the elevator and they hear it, they might pretend they don't, but what if one person turns and looks at you and says, "That is disgusting". Is the belch any different? Nope, same tummy gas escaping, but because someone commented, now we have a story in our head – embarrassed or distressed or annoyed. Remove the part that judges (in this case, the elevator passenger) and what is left? What is there to judge? For me, these mental gymnastics helps me realize that the belch or the other person are not problems, they are just...there, input that I don't have to attach to. So, when I tell an existing partner I am going to start dating someone and they say "Eww, really, I thought you had better taste than that", I don't have to attach to the idea I'm being judged or attacked.

TOOL #8 – MANAGING SURPRISES

Dan says...

I once started a relationship and not wanting my current partner to be worried about it, I told her we are just dating but it wouldn't go anywhere. Fast forward twelve years and we all own a house together....

One of the polyamory mistakes I made a lot in the beginning was being protective of my partners. That doesn't sound like a mistake, it sounds like a kind and generous way to be. But the way I did it was problematic. Specifically, I didn't want anyone to have hurt feelings, so I would minimize or not share small details that I didn't think mattered. But of course, those small details make up part of the story, so one day your partner hears you are 'occasionally dating for sexy time' and then to them suddenly you are planning a 4-day romantic cruise.

We call this tool Managing Surprises. That means we do our best to limit those moments that suddenly our partners are faced with something they had no expectation was coming. Now, life is fluid and changes in the blink of an eye and surprises will happen, but often we can take steps to avoid unnecessary surprises. This is easiest to handle by sharing often and without reservation of how anyone might take that information. Once you get into the habit of communicating like this, it gets easier – and is the key to managing those surprises. So instead of one day you are telling your existing partners that you are doing a weekend away with the guy you had coffee with a month ago, be free with the progress – we have started texting, we shared some pictures of our cats, we are on each other's Google Calendar. And the one that helped me the most was that it was ok to say, "I don't know". Meaning that when I was thinking that a new relationship might be something special, but I wasn't sure yet, I let me partner know exactly that – "It might be great, but it might be nothing". This counters the story a partner might tell themselves – "you never talk about that person, so I guessed nothing was happening".

Dawn says...

The management of surprises by partners may not be important or necessary to some, but for me, it's very important. When something sneaks up on me, like a 4-day romantic cruise with someone that I thought my partner was just 'dating', it feels like secrets were kept. I don't usually care, for the most part, what is done on a date or with their time together, except for the fact that it will give me clues on how serious their relationship may be, but I personally need to know how their relationship is progressing so that I can prepare myself for any weird emotions I might have.

And I'm perfectly ok with 'I don't know'. I'd actually prefer that answer rather than to minimize what it is so that my perceived feelings aren't hurt. Treat me like a big girl and tell me the truth. If I have issues with the truth, then those are my issues to deal with. If you aren't telling me the truth, even if it's to protect my feelings, then I will feel lied to through deception.

Secrets, deception, and rejection are big triggers for me. I'm learning how to work with them and to get to a place of equanimity, but it can be challenging. So, we've learned to overshare and to speak the unspeakable. It can cause a little drama right off the bat, or not, but is so much easier to deal with in the long run and helps build that trust that I need in a relationship.

My poor boyfriend - because I need this oversharing in my life, I think everyone needs it. He does not need me to overshare, just to keep him apprised of any new relationships. I do my best to keep anything from being a total surprise to either of my partners. Crud. I have to go tell one of them something now. I've told 2 of them something new, not the third.....damn, be right back...

So, that can be a challenge as well. Did I tell all my partners, or at least the ones that want to know?

Once the trust is built, they have come to understand that if I did forget to tell one of them, it wasn't done on purpose. My intent is to keep everyone informed. Unfortunately, my memory doesn't always follow my plans.

TOOL #9 – MANUAL MODE

Dawn says...

I can remember the first time I consciously used this tool. I was sitting on the floor in the living room and Dan was sitting on the couch. He told me that he was thinking about doing something with the girlfriend. Not that he did it, but that he was thinking about it. In the past, I would instantly feel uncomfortable, betrayed even and would pretty much respond with 'excuse me?' or 'what the fuck?' or 'how could you?'. My instant thought would be 'What about me?' or 'did you think of how this would affect me?'. Which is my clue phrase that I've been triggered, and then the thought would be loud, louder, loudest, out of control. I'd process out loud about how he was hurting me, didn't care about me, why should he care about me, he wasn't listening, everything was about what he wanted, and of course he was going to leave me. It was bad. As an external processor, usually whatever first enters my head as a response, falls out of my mouth, whether it is based on truth or not.

I felt guilty for always reacting like that. It got to the point where he wouldn't want to share things with me because of my reactions. And that would make it worse because then I would feel like he was keeping secrets. Instead, it was just that he was tired of the emotional battles every time he brought something up about a poly partner.

So, this time, I took a breath and just sat there. I paid attention to the ball of fear in the pit of my belly and paid attention to how the rest of my body was reacting and how my mind was reacting. I stayed quiet for a moment. Dan was concerned. This wasn't normal for me. He touched my shoulder and asked if I was ok. I said yes and that I was in 'manual mode' and would explain in a minute.

As an internal processor, I think he got what I was saying.

I took this time to breathe, realize the feeling in the pit of my stomach was a result of a trigger and worked on calming down my emotions so that they would line up with my logic. My logic is, we are poly and of course he's going to date others and do new things with those he's dating. My emotions were screaming, 'of course he's dating others, look at who he's stuck with'. I'd have to talk my emotions down. 'Calm down, look at the logic. He's not stuck with you. He can walk away at any time. He chooses to be with you AND date others, just as you can.' This helped so much. I'd have the conversation with myself before automatically dumping it all over him.

He watched. He watched the expressions on my face. I could tell he was concerned, so I closed my eyes. I had a strong desire to lash out in fear and anger, but a stronger desire to handle some of these emotions on my own instead of attacking him and putting him on the defense.

It worked! I was able to take another breath and look up at him. Wanting to take care of me, he asked me what happened. I told him that a friend of mine had taught me this trick that was taught to her by her therapist. I had explained to her that I was tired of the verbal vomit I was constantly throwing at him any time I felt uncomfortable or triggered (2 totally different things).

I really wish I had learned this tool earlier in our relationship. As with most of our tools, the earlier they are figured out, the more useful they can be.

It's all about taking a quiet break to think about things before speaking. Not suppressing, that's different. I'm also not bashing external processing. There is nothing wrong with being an external processor. I was just tired of yelling and feeling out of control. I was tired of yelling at my partner who was just trying to live his authentic self and create space for me to live my authentic self.

I do want to throw out there that my triggers are based on past experiences with other people and past baggage, not from anything Dan has done. So, I always felt guilty when I responded like that. He hasn't done anything wrong. We are poly, we do poly things.

My responses would drive us both crazy until this little tool was given to me.

Now, instead of having an instant response when I feel that trigger in the pit of my belly, I recognize that that feeling in my belly is a trigger and not based on reality, which means that I've got a moment to make a different decision on how I respond. I will usually sit, take a deep breath and go into my head. In my head I remind myself that he would never do anything to intentionally harm me. He loves me. We are poly. We do poly things. If something breaks because of this new decision of his, he will do his best to fix it. I continue to breathe.

At first, it concerned him when I got quiet instead of lashing out like normal. He thought I was detaching, which is a bad thing for me. I now use the words 'manual mode' when he asks me if everything is ok. He knows that means that I'm processing internally instead of out loud and I'll be ready to talk to him more logically in a little bit, however long a 'little bit' is.

This has been a tremendous help with our communication style. Now he's not concerned about being attacked when bringing up a new subject, I'm not attacking, and he doesn't have to prepare to go on the defensive every time we discuss something new.

Now, with 'manual mode' I usually use a couple more tools, like: WAM, mantra and meditation. We'll talk about them separately.

Dan says...

I must admit, there are times when I wish I would have kept my mouth shut. Not because I should not speak – we are big fans of the idea you should share your word, but sometimes what comes out of my mouth is colored in anger or fear and instead of saying 'I didn't realize you were going out tonight, this is taking me off guard' it comes out as "Whatever, I don't give a shit" when actually, I do.

I don't want to lash out in anger or speak out in selfish rebuke. Meditation (addressed elsewhere in this book) helps a lot. Manual mode also can help with creating a more constructive response.

For me, it is for those times when we want to let both our heart and our mind have a voice. It is for when I am bothered emotionally that a partner is, for example, on a date, but I want to give myself a moment to think about it. I take a few breaths, acknowledge my feeling, and then give my intellectual self a chance to have a say. My brain might pipe up with the fact that we are polyamorous, that I was told about a date or lover (and remind me that I said "great, have a good time" and meant it), and after digging around a bit decides that there is no logical reason for it to bother me. Now, this doesn't mean my feeling is invalid! It only is a check in to say, 'Do I have a reason to be bothered'. Personally, I think 'thank you brain' and go back to the heart, to the feeling, and explore what the feeling actually is. Perhaps my first thought was anger at being betrayed. I now invite logic in and say 'Well, you are not being betrayed, so what is behind that feeling?'. This often leads me to understand that my initial feeling was masking something else – an initial feeling of anger was masking a feeling of fear or loneliness for example.

If I have kept silent as I process this, when I do communicate, it is done without shouting or overreacting, but instead, with the genuine issue or challenge I am facing. And that gives me (and a loving partner) opportunity to find solutions. Maybe now I can say "I didn't realize you were going out tonight, this is taking me off guard, would you mind checking in with me when you know how late you'll be out? I feel kind of vulnerable tonight so am going to hang out with a friend".

TOOL #10 – WORK FROM A PLACE OF ASSISTANCE

Dan says...

As Dawn and I started our relationship, we decided in the very beginning that we would not have a standard relationship and that dating, emotional connection, and sex with other people were all going to be part of the relationship.

As I started to date new people and told Dawn about them, I could see in her reaction that she felt concerned that I would leave her, or that she wasn't enough, or the many other initial reactions that people have when starting polyamory. I made a mistake at that point that took us a long time to figure out. Before I tell you about the mistake, let me share the background of why I made it.

I am of a nature to protect the people I love. There is nothing wrong with that and some would even suggest it is a sign of love that you want to keep those dear to you safe from harm. The problem is when the protection you provide is part of the problem. Here is where we talk about the mistake I made.

In seeing Dawn feeling bad/confused/hurt ("harmed") by me bringing in a new partner, I tried to protect her by getting rid of the new partner. This behavior not only slowed down our polyamory progression but was pretty disrespectful to the new person (and the type of behavior that gives 'unicorn hunters' a bad name). Now, that isn't to say that there isn't a time to evaluate a new partners impact on everyone and possibly decide it is not a fit - after all, any relationship I am in can impact others. But in this case, Dawn never asked me to get rid of anyone. I assumed that course of action. All she wanted from me - and to be honest she asked for, but I could not hear - was to be a good partner and help her process and work through the feelings, to support her in her struggle. This is where the tool 'Work from a place of assistance' came from.

Sometimes when a partner says "you have another new girlfriend? Great, I guess no time for me!" they are not asking you to do anything different, but instead to sit down, give them time and attention, and to simply hear them, to listen with compassion and love, to be a good partner. It may include being a sounding board and offering feedback or thoughts or simply to re-emphasize that they are still important or to just listen and offer a hug. Regardless, it is to avoid taking it personally that they are hurting or to try to prevent them from hurting - instead, simply be with them regardless of what they are feeling. Use the phrase 'How can I help you through this?' or something similar that makes it clear you want to be involved and assist.

Dawn says...

I'm glad I had this conversation with Oberon Zell (his wife Morning Glory Zell coined the term 'polyamory' and I had a chance to talk with him at a Pagan Clergy conference). During the conversation I asked him if it was acceptable to ask a partner for help because I had been doing so and it felt like it was the wrong thing to do. He looked me square in the eye and said, "Partners are partners and they are supposed to help each other".

I shared this conversation with Dan, and we started putting it into play with earnest while Dan was dating others. It was a good thing we did, because once I found someone that I really cared for and fell in love with, and Dan was having his own emotional WAM moments (discussed elsewhere in the book), I had more of a clue of how to handle the situation.

He was driving in the snow one night and the car slipped but Dan was able to keep us on the road, I congratulated him and then went into a story about how Raymond had to do the same thing the other night while we were on our way to a swing club. I felt Dan's emotional hiccup. I felt it half way through the short story but decided not to stop the story. I ask him not to 'protect' me from what he does with others, so I was not going to do that with him.

After the story, I asked him if he was ok. He replied, 'No, I just had a WAM moment.' I asked him if there was anything I could do to help. He thought about it and said, "no". He was working it out but appreciated my offer. I let him know that if he needed anything from me after he processed, to let me know.

That's my way of working from a place of assistance. Anytime I share something, I keep an eye out to see if there was a blip. I don't expect them, but am aware they could happen, so that I can be there to help.

We've made so much progress since recognizing this step was needed for us to process some things that happen. It doesn't mean that we are responsible for the other person's emotions, but it does allow us to be supportive partners to each other.

TOOL #11 - FAIR VS EQUAL

Dan says...

One year, Karen and I took a five-day cruise for vacation. It was great! Being able to unwind, a very lax agenda, room service, romantic meals by moonlight, just a fantastic experience. When we returned, Dawn was happy to see me and, after letting me go on about what a great time I had, she said she had something she wanted to talk about, and (using the tool Draft Email that is elsewhere in this book), she shared with me she didn't like it that she and I never went away on cruises, and that I didn't treat our relationship equal to the way I treated my relationship with Karen. And she was right...but that was the way it should be. See, I used to think that I should treat all my partners equally, but in truth, at least for us, polyamory isn't equal, and we are happiest when we don't try to make it equal, instead, it just needs to be fair.

The cruise I mentioned above is a great example of this. I did take Karen on a five-day cruise and I don't take Dawn on cruises like that. But Dawn and I travel at least fifteen times a year for three-day weekends, presenting classes and workshops in different locations around North America and we enjoy the heck out of doing that - so much so that these 'working trips' all feel like mini-vacations to us. So, although Dawn and I could take a 5-day cruise, it would be at the cost of us doing something that we really enjoy.

Each situation and relationship is different. Although we might have an initial reaction to try to fight for equal, instead we try to figure out what we actually want, regardless of what someone else is experiencing. We realize that if sometimes we are arguing that 'since he got ice cream, I want ice cream too!', but when we step back and ask, do we actually want ice cream, we may realize we actually prefer cake or pie or going on cruises. We ask ourselves if our only motivation is because someone else got (it).

In the case of Dan and Dawn and Karen, fair is I take time to cultivate our two-person relationship with both Karen and Dan, and Dawn and Dan. The shape that takes, in general, is different. When we take time away for a few days the activity – be it a cruise, camping, presenting, exploring coffee shops, live action role play games, or staying at home and binging on some TV show – needs to reflect what we as that coupling enjoy.

For us, the most important aspect isn't the 'what' we are doing but that of simply focused time. Often what a partner wants isn't an activity at all – it is just being with you.

Dawn says...

There really isn't a way to have 'equal' relationships. Each relationship is different and... I like it that way. If they were all the same, I don't think it would be as much fun.

We can make them fair. Though, each relationship will have its own idea of what is fair, and fairness doesn't always get compared to other relationships.

For example, if Raymond and his wife drive across the country to spend time with their kids, do I really expect something 'equal'? What would be 'equal'? Him and I driving across the country to visit his kids? Why would we do that? And what else would make it equal? There is no reason for us to take a 5-day trip. There is no reason for him to have to do something with me that would be a 'tit for tat'. Our relationship doesn't involve doing 5-day trips and doesn't need to. If it happens, it happens, but it doesn't need to out of some sense of 'equal'.

There are things Raymond does with me that he doesn't do with his wife and she doesn't need or want him to do them with her. There are things I do with Raymond that I don't do with Dan and vice versa.

Instead, we work on the relationship and do what makes sense for the relationship. That's what is fair.

TOOL #12 – PORCH TIME

Dan says...

I used to really have some less than nice thoughts about one of my partner's partners. I thought they were slimy at best, but my partner loved this person. So, was I supposed to share this feeling? Stuff it? How would I feel if someone told me that my choice in a romantic partner was poor?

One of the most common things Poly people say is 'You must communicate!'. But sometimes, they just leave it at that and assume that everything from how much you envy a new guys great physical shape to how much you hate a metamour is something you just randomly jump into.

We developed a tool sometime back which has been a polyamory lifesaver for those "tough conversations". It is called Porch Time. It is for those times you need to talk really openly without worry about offending the other person and is valid for anything from the heavy earth-shaking topics to just something you need to vent about. To start off, you tell the person you want to talk to that you want "Porch Time". For this tool to work, the other person only responds with 'Ok'. It is preferable that you talk right then, although it isn't always possible. If you need to set a date and time, do so, otherwise, find a spot away from others and away you go.

At its minimum, Porch Time is a chance to vent without fear of reprisal. It is a neutral space where we can express ourselves without any role, preconceived notion of our relationship, or previously defined label. This is the place where when other communication methods didn't work, we had a 'free space' to fall back on where everything - bitching, whining, yelling, complain, screaming, and crying are all fair game. We could call each other names if that was the emotional need, and the key was for us all was the core understanding that humans are emotional creatures and sometimes it is the act of verbalizing fear or frustration that allows us to get to where we need to process it, and the ability of our partners to honor that and to not hold it against us later.

Dawn says...

For us, it was literally a porch, a very tiny porch at our apartment.

We had never really learned to communicate successfully in our past marriages and needed a tool where we could get everything out instead of bottling it up. Transparency was one of our needs in our relationships and holding in emotions is not being transparent. So, we decided that instead of arguing in front of the kids, cat and dog, we'd go out onto the porch and dump it all out.

What ended up happening is that that porch became our safe and sacred space where we could literally talk about and say anything. We could yell if it was needed, we could vent and stomp our feet. We could externally process until we came to a spot where we hit the truth of our emotions.

What started out as a 'you, you, you', would settle down and become an 'oh, crap, I have work to do on me' moment. But, by creating this sacred space and holding space for each other, with the goal of finding a resolution, we were able to rip apart some of these emotional upheavals and find the core of what really was going on.

We considered this one of our tools for personal growth, and the kids saw us doing this. They saw us requesting porch time from each other, heard us going outside and arguing or having loud conversations, heard it calm down. Saw us walk back inside holding hands and feeling much calmer. They asked us what we talked about out there, and we told them 'anything that was upsetting us or may upset the other person and we can't punish each other for it.' They liked the idea that they couldn't get punished for whatever was brought up, that it was a safe space, so they started using porch time with us.

I can remember one son getting a bad grade and he asked for porch time before telling us about it. He was able to share. We listened and before leaving the porch, a plan of action was put into place instead of 'punishment'. Knowing they could do this in the future, kept them from trying to keep secrets from us because they were afraid of hurting our feelings or getting punished.

Over time, the kids grew up and we learned other methods of communication, so haven't used porch time in many years, but I still value the idea that it's available to me if I need it. It's also available to any of my partners that want to use it.

Now, porch time may not sound like something you want to use. That's fine. Like some of our tools, it's not for everyone, but what I do recommend is that you come up with a communication tool that works for you. Our goal was for there to never be a reason for a partner to say, 'but I didn't know how to tell you.'

TOOL #13 - MANTRA

Dawn says...

Have you ever been so triggered when your partner has been out with someone else that you can't handle yourself emotionally? I have gotten that worked up before. I'd be so sad and so scared that he was going to find someone else that he liked more than me and leave me. Low self-esteem, I know. Crap from my childhood, I know, but these emotions were real. Then, I'd be afraid that if leaving wasn't in his head before, it would definitely be there now because of how emotional I was.

It would just tear me up and I wouldn't be able to get through the trigger. I can remember driving trying to work through the emotions. My head would feel like spaghetti as I tried using the tools that I had learned, but sometimes they wouldn't work. I'd be so wrapped up in my fear that driving was scaring me, and I knew that I had to pull myself out of it. I couldn't call anyone because I wouldn't make any sense. My partner was usually my anchor when I got triggered, but the fact that he was out with someone else is what had triggered this loss of control, so I didn't feel like I should reach out to him while he was on a date because that would interrupt his date, which wasn't fair to him or the other person.

So, to get myself under control, I had to simplify. My brain just couldn't untangle the spaghetti thoughts. I needed something that it could anchor to, something simple. Over time, my mantra was born.

I can remember saying to myself, trying to calm myself down, 'I know he loves me. I trust him, and I trust our relationship and I trust that we were put together for a reason. I also have faith in what we've built together, and I have no reason to fear that he'll leave me.' I can remember trying to say that over and over again, but as I did, it got shorter and shorter. It finally because, 'Love, Trust, Faith'. I would say it over and over again until I calmed down. It worked!

After creating that mantra, it was used many times; sometimes I would say it over and over until I calmed down. As I became more stable with my emotions over time, I'd only have to say it a couple of times to anchor myself.

So, that's my mantra with Dan. I also have another one with my boyfriend. I can remember telling him that I knew I would get jealous if he started dating someone else, or when I asked him if he'd have any issues if I started dating someone else.

54

Both times, he looked at me confused and said, 'we are poly, this is what we do.' I love this saying and have turned it into my second mantra.

If either of my partners want to date someone else, or change the relationship with a current partner, my response is, 'we are poly, this is what we do', and it helps so much.

I don't know how many people have inner voices that talk as fast as mine does, but if it's allowed to it will go off on a tangent and it's hard to capture and hold down before it gets totally out of control with weird stories. So, having a mantra, a phrase or a couple of words to anchor to, is very powerful.

Dan says...

Mantra meditation is intended to help to alter your state of consciousness. The mantras we are sharing here are no different – to take what you are currently stuck in and give yourself some time to breathe and not be trapped in it. Sometimes my feelings and thoughts are like that - traps. I'll find a situation and it becomes a "chicken and the egg" situation – did some thought cause emotional turmoil? Or is the emotional turmoil feeding unskillful thoughts? It doesn't matter where it comes from, one will power the other, and it spins out of control.

A mantra can be that anchor that gives us a moment to breathe and stop things from spiraling down. But making my foremost thought our mantra (for me, I've gone through a few, but the one that sticks with me now is – and all due credit to Stranger in a Strange Land – "Waiting is"). I start to play out the drama in my head and my heart starts to feel shitty and the drama gets worse and I, at some point, bring *'Waiting Is' to my thoughts and start to catch those worrisome thoughts and counter with Waiting Is. And notice my belly is tight or heart is racing and breathe and think (or whisper) Waiting Is. And eventually, I smile and realize that I've been here before....and all my stories are normally wrong to one degree or another and I should chill until I know what is.

The concept around "Waiting Is", is that sometimes we don't know all the facts and need more data before we can formulate an opinion. But we - people - are not good at that patience thing so we get stressed, reckless search for clues where there are none, and start making up things to fit the gap. Instead, recognize that it isn't time to decide. Relax, let things play out, and go from there.

TOOL #14 - CHANGE THE STORY

Dawn says...

Have you ever had those moments of 'he didn't answer my email, maybe he doesn't like me anymore' or 'she's going out with him again tonight, she must like him more than me' or a number of other things that we convince ourselves are true... for whatever reason?

Sometimes I totally believe what it is that I'm thinking. So much so that it physically hurts. Sometimes, I know that logically these thoughts aren't true, but emotionally they still feel true. I have had those moments; I have had those moments too many times to count.

'If he's taking her on a cruise, she must be a better traveling companion, or he'd be taking me again.' That's one of my most recent ones.

Oh wait, no, my most recent one...'if he really loved me, he'd call me more'.

At some point in our lives, we all tell ourselves stories that aren't necessarily true. We experience life through our own filters and our own experiences, and that means that sometimes we make assumptions about other people's motives based on our own experiences.

After learning to meditate, which we'll talk about later, my thinking slowed down enough that I could catch myself telling myself stories during meditation and could stop them. Whoa! What a concept. I could stop thinking about stories that weren't necessarily true? Not only could I stop stories, but I could change them.

I had already learned that I could think about outcomes, and even if I thought of 100 outcomes that could happen, it was usually the one I hadn't thought of that really happened. So, why waste time stressing about outcomes that more than likely won't happen? Why waste all that energy?

So, once I learned to stop stories during meditation, and learned how to regulate my emotional responses with 'manual mode'.... I was able to start changing the stories that would flit through my head. Ok, sometimes it wasn't flitting but instead a steel grip of attachment to the story.

Instead of wondering why I didn't get a text response right away....'oh, he must be in the middle of sex with her', or 'oh, I must not be important enough for him to respond'......I would try to think of the things that are true instead. What is it that I know? All I know is that my text hasn't been responded to. Actually, I don't even have proof of that. Truly all I know is that I don't SEE a response. With the basic info in hand, I then picture what is more than likely happening. Maybe he's driving and shouldn't be checking his texts. Maybe his phone is in his pocket and not on vibrate. Maybe he left it in the car. Maybe he's in a meeting. There are so many possibilities; it doesn't have to be a negative reason.

Instead of wondering why she's dating someone new and believing it's because you aren't good enough.... what is that you know? All you know is that she is dating someone new. So, change the story. It's not because she wants the new person 'instead of' but 'along with' you.

When I do this.... it's to build up my confidence in what we've built. If I keep thinking everything is happening because of negative reasons, there isn't going to be any joy in my poly. If you can't stop the stories, then at least turn them into neutral or positive ones. It's a way of rewiring your thought process.

Now I catch myself changing the story all the time. My goal is to have positive thoughts first, instead of having to change the negative story to a neutral or positive one. I'm finding that this does happen over time.

Dan says...

I used to have stories start (anything from 'They are probably holding hands as they walk' to 'they are probably having The Sex right now') and find myself getting worked up, upset and jealous and angry, and try to shut down the story. Unfortunately, that only made it stronger. Those stories would creep out instead when I was almost asleep or was otherwise 'off guard', and that felt bad – I didn't want to feel like I had to be on guard at all – I wanted to move from tolerating my partners other relationships to accepting, from accepting to rejoicing. But that can't happen if I am constantly feeling like I must protect myself from what my partners are doing that is outside of me.

So, instead of rejecting the story, I started to...well, to mentally direct that story. The best example I have of this is when one of my partners started to have intimate time with a new person in their life and I caught myself trying to avoid thinking about it. I found myself pushing away the images that came to mind and decided to instead bring the images to mind. What would it look like? It was very...well, visual. I pictured him fingering her, on top of her, the contrast of their skins. It wasn't pornographic, and it didn't turn me on. But I did have to think 'how was she feeling?'. Well, in my story, she was feeling good – great even – and enjoying herself, and in that moment, I was happy for her. Sex is fun and enjoyable and why wouldn't I want her to feel enjoyment? The difference was that I wasn't part of the story. I wasn't excluded – I just wasn't there, and since it wasn't about me and separated from "What about me?", it was just a nice love story, and about pleasure for someone I cared about.

TOOL #15 – COMPARING SEX

Dan says...

I happen to have sex with people who have sex with other people. Specifically, the two people I currently sleep with most often also sleep with other people. My other partners have sex with a variety of other people, male and female.

When I started having sex with a sexually active partner, there was a time of feeling threatened by such a situation. After all, what if (the other person they are having sex with) is better at it than me? Perhaps, if they were a guy, they were bigger, or had better stamina, or knew things I did not, even was able to last till just the right moment? And thus, my partner would prefer this other lover perhaps and I would have a reduced amount of sex, and believe it or not, worse in my head, was a reduced amount of respect. Because from my high school chums to modern media, I've been taught if you cannot satisfy your partner better than anyone else, you are not a "real man". And that a "real man" will come along and take that lover away (I have been told by female identifying partners they deal with a version of this as well).

With this thought in mind, when it came time to make love, I would subconsciously (and sometimes consciously) bring these other partners to bed and try to 'beat them', to win at being the best lover. This was both a doomed idea, as well as a stupid one. One that benefited those external partners by making them better lovers! It was a doomed attempt because my level of control over some of my physical attributes is limited. Although there are things that you can do on a physical level to assist you in being a better lover, there are some things you cannot affect. The size and shape of your prick or pussy is what it is. You might be able to make some adjustments (some parts are more malleable than other parts) but overall, when it comes down to it, you got what you got.

My cock is exactly some number of inches and has a slight downward curve. So, if a slight downward curve is not as enjoyable to you as 45-degree angle up, then, so be it. No penis pump or set of clamps will change what is.

And it was a stupid attempt not because I wanted to be a better lover, but because I was trying to be better than someone else. My mind would be on 'how can I pleasure better than' - and this was a thought process that directly disempowered the very thing that I (and my partners) most cherish in sexual connections; the physical + emotional + spiritual aspects that make sex a complete sensual union.

That fully connected state is what makes it more than just two people humping, more than just a physical thing. It was not stupid to desire to be a better lover. It was the path of comparing myself to another that was in error, instead of simply cultivating being more of a lover.

There came a point where I was able to surrender the war on myself (I was the only one telling me stories of my failures). Once I recognized it, I realized that no one was a better lover than us, and no one was a worse lover than us. Because us cannot be compared to our partners and their partners. It is a different situation and a different experience.

To expand upon the concept of "Us", you need only realize that you are an entity upon yourself, you are you. And you are the only one of your kind. And your partner is him/her, and they too are one of a kind, an individual like none other. And your partners other partners, or your other partners, by that same view, are again all separate and original and no one else is exactly like them. If that is so, then this must be so as well - that you (an entity unlike anyone else) plus your partner (a likewise individual) create an Us unlike any other. I view it as the Us entity, a third co-created being if you will, that only exists in the joining of two individuals. And since the Us cannot be duplicated, and the Us that is created via a partner and anyone else, then there is no reason to attempt to be more or better, as there is in truth two different things that cannot be replicated.

When a partner and I make love, and we create the new entity of Us, that is a sacred being that simply cannot be duplicated. A fool errand to try. And disingenuous. My lovers love me - the sex, the contact, the interaction, the dance we have when we are between the sheets. That is what draws us together. It is not skill, but connection. And although I will never be able to replicate what my partner does with her partner, they will never be able to duplicate what we do, and that is just how it should be. Thus, comparison of partners and sexual skill might be interesting to discuss, there is great folly in trying to duplicate it. Instead, create your own Us.

Dawn says...

I can remember having sex with Dan and wondering what it was that he found interesting in his other partners. I mean, our sex is so damn good! But what if he was more interested in what he had with his other partners? I had nothing left to

60

give; I was giving it my all, being totally open and honest and letting my passion flow freely. I allowed myself to be vulnerable. What else could I do?

Well, what I could do was to take Dan's advice when I talked to him about this. What he says above is absolutely right, I needed to drop my attachment to what my other partners do with their other partners. All I have is me. All I can be is me and that's good enough.

My sexual relationships are each very different. They are because the people involved are different. The sex that Raymond and I have is different than what he and Julie have. The sex that any of us have is different because what we create together is different. We blend differently.

More of this made sense when I had sex with Raymond for the first time. Again, as I've stated throughout the book, Dan had other partners on his own before I did. So, it took me longer to figure out.

So, it's not that sex with another partner is 'better', but it's definitely different, and isn't that part of the fun of it? Just be yourself and the blending of the different energies of persons will create its own Us.

Know that your partners are creating something completely different than what the 2 (or more) of you have together, and even what you have with just yourself is going to be completely different than what you have with another person.

TOOL #16 – ANCHORS

Dawn says...

Sometimes when I'm feeling emotional, I'll turn to my ancient teddy bear for comfort. I mean, this poor bear is ancient. There are photographs of me just at the age of walking and holding onto this teddy bear at a Christmas tree. So, I'm assuming I've had him since I was 1 ½ years old. The poor guy has seen better days, but he has always made me feel safe and comforted.

He is one of my anchors.

An emotional anchor is an object (usually) that anchors us in the storm. These objects can anchor us to a state of mind, bring us comfort, ground us, remind us that we are in the present.

My teddy bear was there through troubled times and made me feel like someone loved me. He was truly my go-to for comfort and now, he sits by my bed on a shelf on a soft blanket my grandmother made for me, and if I'm really feeling the need, I curl up in bed with him and can fall asleep, usually after crying on his shoulder.

He's been brought down off the shelf more than once during my journey into polyamory and I'm sure he'll be my comfort again in the future.

Another anchor I used to use is a beautiful rose quartz Kwan Yin pendant. She started out as a necklace and then when the chain broke, she hung out in my pocket or my purse. Now, she sits on my altar in my meditation room.

An anchor can be anything, including an animal. We used to have a cat, Dusty. He was a beautiful, soft fluffy Blue Persian. When I came home from a hard appointment with my therapist, Dusty would be waiting for me at the door, and as soon as I would sit on the couch, he'd be in my lap, purring and snuggling with me. He didn't do this too often, but he certainly did it if he knew I was upset, which was usually after one of those appointments. He was absolutely an anchor that was very grounding.

So, whether it's a treasured object from the past, something that brings a good memory from the present, a stone, a pet, or something personal, it can be an anchor in the storm. Pull it out and spend time with it. Breathe. And feel the emotions calm down so that you can release the pain and the fear.

TOOL #17 - 48 HOUR RULE

Dan says...

Once when Dawn came home from a date and she started to tell me about how great it was, she suddenly stopped and asked, "Is everything ok?". I smiled (or perhaps gritted my teeth) and said "Yep, it's fine, go on..." and she went on with her story and at the end, she again asked me, "Is something wrong?".

Our most serious, intense, and emotional arguments have come about after we began to try polyamory. I'm not telling you that to scare you off of poly (although let's face it, it isn't a selling point). Although Dawn and I argued before we started practicing polyamory, we did what many couples do; when a touchy subject came up, we skirted around it and let it pass. With polyamory, that just doesn't work. You must face those tough subjects so that you can make progress and move beyond them.

We have a few agreements we hold to so that when we do argue, we don't fight. One of those is the "48-hour rule". There are a few aspects that make up this tool. First, if you ask me what is wrong, and I say nothing, then you trust me that nothing is wrong, which means I can't count on you to read between the lines or guess, and my passive behavior "NOTHING" gets ignored. This is valuable because it forces me to take responsibility for my emotional state and to speak my truth - if something is wrong, I have to say so. If I say "Nothing", then you should go on about the day as if nothing is wrong, even if I am lying.

This isn't to be cold or to ignore me - it is to set the requirement that we must learn to speak up when we need to. But for this to work, there is another answer that I can give - instead of "nothing", I can say "Yes, but I don't want to discuss it now", because sometimes something is wrong, but I don't want to talk about it yet. It might be that I am upset and don't want to speak from anger, or that I need some time because I am an internal processor, maybe that I just don't feel like dealing with it right then. So, it is fine if I say "Yes, something is wrong, but not ready to discuss it".

Now, often Dawn will ask "Is it me?" and I'll say 'no, just need to chew on it' and that is the end of the conversation...for now. This is where the 48 hours part comes in. I have 48 hours to bring it up and address it - and if I don't, then I have to let it go and it is over. That means we don't get to use something that happened four years ago as ammo for a current argument. Instead, when I am ready to talk about it, I let the person I want to talk to know and we grab a chair and have a chat.

Dawn says...

I was married before. In this relationship, if someone did something that pissed the other person off, we held on to that. We didn't talk about it. We waited until one of us blew up and then every resentment we had shoved in our back pocket was pulled out and used to attack the other person. This was done by both of us, and I hear that many other relationships use this same method for arguments. I remember a woman at work talking about something that had happened with her husband that morning and that she was putting that in her back pocket for their next argument. The other women agreed that that is what they did as well. I heard that and was really glad that we had come up with a different solution. Who wants to hold on to that stuff?

Also, Dan is an internal processor, and because of this I needed him to have a sort of code word like '48 hours' to make sure that he wasn't shoving stuff down just so that he wasn't hurting my feelings. And if he was processing, I needed to know that he had 48 hours to bring it up, otherwise it would feel like he was holding onto secrets. Then, I had to let it go. I had to let the stories go and trust him to bring it up if he needed to.

I'm sensitive to others' emotions and can usually tell when something is wrong. With the 48-hour rule, if I ask him if something is wrong, he can either speak up if there is, or say not there isn't, or say he needs time to process before talking. If his reply is the latter, I know we'll talk again in the next 48 hours, so I don't need to keep asking him if something is wrong. I can give him the time and space he needs to process whatever is going on, otherwise, it felt like he was holding on to secrets. The idea of secrets triggers my PTSD and low-self-esteem issues that I had. What fun that has been.

Having this tool in place has really helped with our communication, and then if we do end up having an argument, there shouldn't be any unresolved issues that get thrown into the mix to confuse things.

TOOL #18 – DRAFT EMAIL

Dan says...

When Dawn is off with another partner – either for a dinner date or a weekend away – I want her to be engaged and attentive to that person. It is important that when she or I is with one of our other partners, we can pay attention to them. So, although we may not mind the occasional text ("Where did u leave the peanut butter?"), having long conversations about the emotional ramifications of the date we are currently on should wait until the date is wrapped up. Yes, I want and expect my partners to be supportive of me, and although I might be feeling distraught, perhaps even 'left behind', I also want to balance giving my partners the courtesy to enjoy their time with another person, hence, we created the Draft Email.

The Draft Email is exactly that – open your favorite email program (or if you prefer, go old school and break out pen and paper), and start writing. The key is to remember that it is just a draft email and that you won't be sending it (although we will return to this in a moment). So, are you feeling a lot of emotional angst? Let it out! Angry and want to lash out? Ok, do it! Is your partner thinking with their cock while you stay home and suffer?

Write it! You are allowed! There are no boundaries...but keep going, and as you keep writing, let your mind start to hear what you are saying. Slowly, as you write, ask yourself if there is a deeper message. Is there another feeling hiding behind the anger and pain? If there is, write that out too. The focus here is to write what you feel, without judging if it is 'right' or 'good' and keep going. Keep going until you have said everything you have to say.

We've found that this kind of an emotional purge can be very valuable in processing our intense feeling selves. It can help you get from a sense of betrayal or terror to a place that feels more honest, more real to you. The emotions – although still there and still weighing on you – are often significantly more manageable.

Here is an import Pro Tip: When creating a draft email, keep the "To" field blank. You don't want to accidentally hit 'send' if sending this message is not the intent....

The next part of this tool is for those poly people who are really interested in working on self-acceptance and growth for themselves and each other is that you all agree that the Draft Email is a valid tool for emotional exploration. That it is not about the other person; it is not an attack of the partner that you are writing about, but it is a processing tool. The way we use the tool in this regard is that when our partner comes home from a date, we first do our best to listen with compersion – did you have a good time, did they have a nice time as well? We do our best to share their joy. And when ready, the 'back from a date' partner makes the offer for us to share our Draft Email if we have one.

We recommend printing that email and, in a place of calm and support, share it with the partner. You establish that "I was hurting, and this is what I felt at that time" and then read it aloud to them, and as you go on, you share where that feeling comes from. Your partner sits in neutrality and doesn't feel judged; they listen as if it is about another person. They realize that this isn't statements of facts; this is a process. Nothing more.

This is really hard and even harsh, but when we master this skill, we learn to accept our own emotions as indicators instead of facts. The only way to deal with the dark stuff is to bring it to the light. And when we have a partner that can sit there and be one with them, even when you seem to be shitting on them ("I heard you say you think I am a selfish bitch; but I heard you later say that you know that we are actually staying to our agreements and not being selfish when you are on a date") then we have great strides available in both personal and relationship growth and bonding.

An example Draft Email for me starts like this (and a small warning, it is pretty intense, raw, and without filter)

"I can't fucking believe you are going out with him. He is a slimy womanizer and the fact you are out with him makes me wonder about you. Jesus fucking Christ are you kidding me? And here I am trying to be a better person and be here for you and canceling my date, so we can have time together and bam you fucking go off with that fuck. I hope you have a great time cause I am sitting here in hell. And hope he is a great lay cause being with you feels pretty revolting right now"

And after some processing gets to...

"Look, I don't really dislike him, I don't even know him, and I know you told me this was coming. But he really is so unlike me I feel like maybe you are looking for someone else. Like are we on the rocks and you want something new and different? Am I boring? And yes, I don't like you having sex with him. To be honest I'm not sure I like you having sex with anyone else sometimes. And I know, I have sex with other people, and I know it doesn't really hurt our relationship. Hell, it makes it better sometimes. Damn it. But let's face it, I am the one home alone. Yeah, I know, I knew this date was coming, and I know better than to sit around in my pity pot. Never has worked before. I don't know I just miss you and want a hug and need to hear I'm still part of things. Love you"

Dawn says...

When we first tell people about the Draft Email as a tool, it can sound harsh, and the words used to start the letter off can be harsh. We are taking these crappy emotions and putting them on paper. They can sound awful, but sometimes this Draft Email can get stuff out on a deeper level than journaling, because we are addressing the person, writing them directly. So, it takes a different tone than writing in a journal, unless that's how you write journals, which isn't a bad idea.

My journaling goes something like this......" Well, tonight I'm sitting here by myself, again. Why? Because he's out with her again. So, why do I feel like this?" ....and goes along on that line. It remains on the surface and is usually asking me questions and trying to answer my questions.

But, if I write a letter 'to' someone, I can point that finger and 'yell'. I can get it all out, everything that is screaming through my head. I can yell and yell and yell and give a focus to all that adrenaline that is filling my body.

I find that if I do that and keep writing beyond that, I get to a sense of calm. Sometimes it's a sense of sadness, sometimes it's a 'where the hell did that come from?" Sometimes it just drains me and I'm able to sleep.

Sometimes it can shock me because I don't want to be the person that has those thoughts, but there it is in black and white. It helps line up my logic and emotions, which brings calmness.

I may share this later, but usually, I find that after I've written it, I don't need to share unless I want to show him how much I've grown from starting to write the letter to how I ended it. Or I like to share what my 'aha' moment was in the writing. I may even remind him not to take it personally, because the writing can be rough. I make sure to focus on the positive points of what writing this letter accomplished.

I don't use this tool so much anymore, as we've built other tools over time that keep me from getting to this emotional point, but that doesn't mean that I won't be using it in the future as we continue to date new people.

TOOL #19 – PERSPECTIVE FROM ANOTHER'S SHOES

Dawn says...

There are a couple of things that I just couldn't grasp at the beginning of this journey. As I've said over and over, I had an issue with jealousy and feeling less than and the fear of rejection that continuously popped up when we started dating separately. For the first five years of this new way of doing poly for us, he was the only one dating. So, it felt like he was the one having fun and I was the only one doing the work.

Then, I got my feet wet and started dating someone myself, which gave me some of my own experiences. These new experiences were really needed to help propel me further in my growth. This person and I broke up and then I fell for Raymond.

As mine and Raymond's relationship grew, I was starting to experience the same stuff that Dan had gone through. I was seeing it from his shoes. I now emotionally understood how he could love me and someone else because I was doing the same. It had always been there emotionally when we dated the same person, and logically when we started dating separately, but it really kicked in when I had my own serious relationship, and it grew from there.

I started seeing things from others' viewpoints; my partners, my partner's partners. Not just seeing but understanding. I started to understand how people wanted me to react to their relationships, because it's how I wanted them to react to mine. I started paying attention to how I reacted to other relationships. It really started to click!

A couple of things happened when I started dating Raymond, and it really made me start paying attention and I did a lot of reflection on my past behavior. For example, I had an opportunity to officiate a wedding in Kentucky. Dan wasn't available, so I thought this would be a great opportunity for Raymond and me to take a long ride and get to know each other a little better.

It struck me that Dan had told me he wanted to do this with a girlfriend a couple years before this and I had had an issue. Take someone across the state line? But, why would you want to do that? Without me? I'm not allowed to tag along? It's that serious? Now, here I was wanting to do the same thing and hoping he wasn't going to have the same sort of reaction, because it really wasn't a big deal. It was a car trip.

So, I crossed my fingers when I told Dan. Of course, he'd already been through this with me and had had a long time to process what happened. He could have turned it on me and made me feel bad for how I reacted when he wanted to do the same thing, but he didn't. He told me to have a good time and was glad that I'd finally learned that it's not as big a deal as we make of things sometimes.

Was it because he truly had compersion? Because he'd already done this with his girlfriend a long time ago? Because he knew how he had wanted me to react to his news and decided to react that way himself to my news? I think it was a combination of all 3.

But, it's the third option that caught my interest. How he reacted to my news felt so good. I took it to him, and he supported me and my relationship with the boyfriend. He was confident and at least seemed to be happy for me/us. Looking back, how many opportunities had I missed where I could have done the same for him?

I told myself I was going to make a point to try and do the same for him, see his perspective from his shoes.

Another thing that happened was that I experienced a metamour (Raymond's wife, Julie) that was truly ok with most anything that Raymond and I wanted to do. I mean, she was really ok with it. She had such confidence in their relationship, that not much fazed her, and she truly wanted him to be happy. I wanted to grow up to be like her (and told her so).

Having Julie be ok with me, lent an energy to our relationship (mine and Raymond's) that was easy going. I wanted to give this gift back to Dan and his other relationships and any other relationships I may develop, and any relationships Raymond might develop. What a gift! There is less tension all the way around; less struggle.

This is the gift that I wanted to pass on. I wanted Dan to feel happy with all his partners, just as the boyfriend was happy with his wife and me because we weren't struggling with each other. So, I decided to emulate my metamour. I'm an introvert and she is an extrovert, so I think it's a little easier for her, but I decided to give it my best effort.

To share this gift with others, I make sure to pause before I have an emotional reaction and ask myself, 'how would I want him to respond if I had just told him the same thing? Wouldn't I want there to be a smile on his face and to have him truly happy that I'm doing something that makes me happy?' of course I would. So, that's what I offer in return. Usually, just thinking this way makes the emotions follow suit. I have intent and will and the emotions follow.

I try to practice this with the metamours as well. When I learn that one of them gets to do something with one of my partners, I remember to ask myself how would I want my metamour to react when they find out that I get to do something with one of their partners? I would want them to be happy that their partner is happy and not be worried about whatever may happen. I'd want them to be confident in themselves and their relationship. So, that's what I try to remember to offer them in return.

It's the same if one of my partners wants to date someone new; I breathe and then think about how I want them to react if I tell them I'm going to be dating someone new. I want them to be excited for me and confident in what we have together. I don't want them to fear that I'm going to replace them, so I offer them this same gift.

Just recently, Dan and I were at a party and Dan had a chance to play with someone. He let me know about it before it happened and then asked if I was ok. I truly was. He was remembering 'old Dawn's' reactions to new situations. Usually, I'd have a hiccup and start asking a lot of questions out of fear. I'm sure he dreaded each time he brought something new to me. But, with this tool, I've been able to turn that around. He let me know about the play date, and I told him to have fun.

He'd met up with someone earlier that day as well, and I asked him what his intentions were. He paused a little, waiting for an 'old Dawn' reaction as he admitted as to what he had in mind. I quickly processed what he told me, remembered I'd want him to be excited for me if I had the same opportunity, put a genuine smile on my face, gave him a hug and told him to have a great time.

What a difference this has made in my life, in all our lives!

Dan says...

Some things that Dawn and I do, Karen does not enjoy, and vice versa. This is a great benefit of polyamory, but lots of things I do with either Karen or Dawn or someone else, many of my partners would have enjoyed, as well. We all share a common interest in board games, coffee shops, and going on trips. So, when I tell Karen that Dawn and I are going on a trip, it can be natural to feel some envy, and the solution, or at least the thing that makes it much easier, is when you can gain the perspective from the other person's shoes. The perspective of the other person can lead to being generous (see the section on Generosity and Graciousness for more on that) and helps overcome selfishness. Once I realized that it was not just about my opportunities, but my partners as well, it all made a lot more sense.

TOOL #20 – BEING WITH POLYAMOROUS PEOPLE

Dawn says...

I recall when we first started poly and going to my monogamous sister and crying on her shoulder. She was so upset for me and so mad at Dan. She expressed this anger and it confused me. I couldn't understand why she was mad at him. He wasn't doing anything wrong, but in her eyes he was. She is very monogamous and doesn't understand us having other partners. She loves me very much but can't understand why we live the way we live, and she wanted to protect her baby sister. "I am lion, hear me roar." I love my sister, but this wasn't helping my situation. (And I know you are reading this book sis, so don't take it personally. I love you for trying and listening to me all those nights on the phone. It did and does mean a lot to me.)

The next time I had the same issue, I decided to spare my sister and went and cried on a friend's shoulder. She got angry at Dan as well and once again I was confused. I wasn't looking for people to take sides, I was just looking for a shoulder to cry on while I tried to work my way through my emotions. Her response was, "Of course you are upset. You should be upset. Dan is dating another woman." That didn't help either, and now I'm upset because I'm upsetting my sister and my friend.

And this was so not the advice I was looking for.

What I needed to hear was that everything was going to be ok, that my feelings were normal and would fade away, or shift as I used my tools (which they did), that I'm not the first one to experience this and I wouldn't be the last. Maybe even share some tools with me that have worked for them or point me towards some resources, not a well-meaning friend trying to convince me that what I really needed was a divorce.

So, now I advise people to go to their polyamorous friends and contacts for support and advice and not just friends that are poly but those with similar styled polyamorous relationships. If you are hierarchical and go to someone that isn't, say a relationship anarchist, or vice versa, the advice still isn't going to be what you need to hear. So, find someone that lives your style or close to it and lives it successfully, you are going to want to hear their words of experience, not theory.

Dan says...

I'll just add that sometimes I don't need advice and counsel. I need people around me, not to talk about relationship or help me process, just to hang out and play a board game. And if the subject comes up that Dawn isn't here because she is on a date, then being around people who will say 'huh, sounds fun' and we keep doing what we are doing, helps me feel normal.

TOOL #21 – WORKING JOURNAL

Dawn says...

As I've pointed out in other parts of the book, there was a time during our polyamorous journey that was really challenging for me. As we started to date others separately, I had a lot of issues with feeling lonely, and not knowing how to be with myself or take care of myself. Sometimes, I'd try to hide it so that he wouldn't have to worry about me, but other times it would just slip out and we'd have to deal with it before his date or after - neither was any fun. So, with both of us struggling with my reactions, I had to come up with another tool that would help with my emotions.

I was used to being with Dan, and the idea that he wanted to be with someone else was a challenge, but it's who we are. We are poly. Though dating separately wasn't our goal when we first started, it only made sense since coamory wasn't working for us.

So, I needed to learn how to take care of myself while he was gone. It was only fair, as he was busy and didn't need to be the one in charge of taking care of me. It's challenging and frustrating. I'm a grown woman. I should know how to take care of myself and work through the pain and the suffering that I'm inflicting on myself, but it's not something I'd learned how to do.

I'd always taken care of other people - my parents, my children, my ex - but not myself. I would ask others what worked for them. People would give me advice, and sometimes it would work and sometimes not. So, being the researcher and writer that I am, I decided to keep track of what did work and what didn't work. I called this my working journal.

A working journal is where I'd document different things I'd try and the results.

For example, I thought that it would be fun to be home on my own and play a video game that we played together. That's what everyone wants, right? Time alone? I figured if I used that time to practice the game, then I'd be ready for him when we played together. Instead, I would cry because I was home alone, playing a video game that we usually played together, and I'd get resentful of having to be home alone. Note in journal, 'Don't stay home alone. It makes you sad', and I would date it, because things can change over time.

Then, I figured that if I couldn't stay home alone, I'd try spending time with some friends. I picked a couple of friends that I really like hanging out with. This only worked sometimes. What I needed to track was when it worked and when it didn't. Usually, what didn't work was when I hung out with my monogamous friends. They loved me, but they just didn't get what I was going through.

Sometimes I'd go to parties in Cleveland, again, sometimes this would work and sometimes it wouldn't. If people asked me 'Where is Dan?', because they were used to seeing us together, it would usually send me in a tailspin, but if I started the conversation with, 'thought I'd come up and spend some time with you guys because Dan is busy', I would usually end up having a good time. So, why was this? I figured it out by writing it down in my physical, handwritten book.

As I grew and changed, sometimes I would try something again that didn't work before. Sometimes it works, sometimes it doesn't; but I made sure to document each occurrence. Over time, I grew through my challenges and don't have many things to document. But I keep the book in case I run into those challenges again with a new partner.

Dan says...

Dawn and I have attended a lot of classes and workshops on polyamory and we often hear a presenter say, "When you experience this, you should do that". They might be recommending something they heard about, or they read about, or that they themselves have tried and found effective.

But all people are different. I'd try to take advice and ideas and sometimes it would work great; other times, it would be ineffective and even feel like a waste of time. And that does not mean it is bad advice - it just means we are all different. Thus, the Working Journal is my way to find out what works for me. When I am in the middle of feeling down or self-pity or just mopey, I get to use this self-created resource for what I know has worked for me. I can see in my own words my own experience that says, "When I felt blue, I tried this thing, and that helped a lot".

TOOL #22 – WAM AND COLLAPSING TRIGGERS

Dawn says...

For me, this is one of those 'aha' tools.

I went through a hard time when Dan split off and started dating on his own, a really hard time - jealous, lonely, feeling rejected, envious, lonely, feeling abandoned, lonely...did I mention feeling rejected and lonely?

We had been doing this together for so long that I felt I had done something wrong and wasn't worthy of his time. I felt that I was being pushed away so that he could go out and have fun with someone else. Forget the fact that we are poly by nature, I didn't want him going out and having fun without me. I didn't want him to forget about me while he was rolling in that 'new relationship energy'. I mean, we were good together, why did he want to go out without me? I had loved our co-amorous agreement. It made me feel safe and loved. Though, I understood why he needed to break out on his own, we just couldn't find anyone that was compatible with both of us.

What happened during this time is that I would spiral into depression. I'm already subject to depression, and this time really fueled it.

I finally got tired of being depressed all the time and was working with a therapist. We figured out that the depression was being caused by a trigger. Dan wasn't doing anything wrong. He was well within our agreements that we had at the time. This was a feeling that I needed to work on, this trigger of rejection.

So, I worked on myself. No one said this would be easy and I knew I was coming into this with my personal baggage dragging behind me.

I started paying attention to the feeling of being triggered whenever he would go out on a new date or wanted to have a little more 'Dan time'. I noticed that whenever that trigger feeling would start in the pit of my belly, a phrase was also going through my head....'What about me?'

'What about me?' is how we came up with the term 'WAM'. When triggered in those situations, I was in a WAM moment. 'What about me?' Why do you want to go out with others? What about me? Why do you want to go on a trip with other people? I thought you liked me? What about me? Why are you taking her on a road trip, a cruise, a trip out of state? What about me?

This became my theme during this time. Though, it was good to recognize that it was a trigger that was leading me to feelings of rejection. What is rejection to me? ...being judged and then left behind. It's the being judged part that was the scariest. Wait. No. It's the whole package – being judged and then him finding someone else that doesn't take so much work in her growth. For me, it's a little different than abandonment. Abandonment is where someone decides to leave. It's about them. Rejection is about me being judged, rejected and then the person decides to leave. It's much more personal.

So now, whenever I start thinking 'What about me'? I look at what is triggering me. I breathe through it and then use one or more of my other tools; manual mode, mantra, journaling, breaking habitual patterns.

That question of 'What about me' with the painful lump in the pit of my stomach, tells me that I'm not working with truth. I'm working with old feelings and fears.

Now I can work on collapsing those triggers. When I notice that I'm thinking 'what about me' and realize that it's not based on the present situation, I can make the decision to release them. This takes practice and will not come automatically but gets easier over time.

I rarely hear that question in my head anymore and I'm now able to separate what is a trigger and what is an actual need that I need to express.

Dan says...

I didn't think I'd have anything to add here...and then I did. It was a few years ago and Dawn was dating a new guy. She told me about how much fun they had at the carnival and I was happy for her; she told me the sex was great and I felt pleased for her there as well.

One winter night we are driving along, and I hit a patch of ice. I kept control of the car, but it was a scary moment where I almost lost control of the car. Dawn said something to the fact that (her new boyfriend) was a really good driver and I got suddenly quiet. She asked me what was wrong, and I muttered "WAM moment". My ego took a hit, expecting to be applauded for my driving skill, and instead, I heard about him. I needed that moment of 'what about me' to realize I too have my own moments of unskillful reaction and they can come when you least expect it.

TOOL #23 – GROUNDING

Dawn says...

Have you ever felt out of control emotionally? Logic can't get a grip because the emotions are in charge? This used to happen to me a lot once I started getting in touch with my emotions. Polyamory can do that to you.

I can remember getting triggered by something - we were at my business at the time, named 'The Room". It was a room on the second floor of a building where a lot of support groups for alternative lifestyles met. That night, I believe it was one of the kink groups that was gathered. and ...well, something happened, flipped my switch and lovely, my emotions were out of control. I really hate this feeling and it's why a lot of these tools were developed. Dan saw what had happened and sent me outside to ground, knowing this is a tool that works dramatically for me.

Grounding is exactly what it sounds like.... it's making a connection to the ground, or Mother Earth, or the Earth's core, or however you want to think of it, so that you feel stable and centered and under control of yourself. I would literally take off my shoes, put my bare feet on the dirt and/or grass and breathe. At this place I also had a tree outside the door. So, I would take off my shoes, lean against the tree and breathe.

Even before 'The Room', I used to work in a building that had a grove of about 8 huge oak trees. I was working in this building when we started dating separately. I would learn something new about their relationship and the feeling would start in the pit of my stomach and my emotions would flip flop and spin out of control. I would get lost in the 'what about me'. This isn't good when you are working and must finish your work day.

So, I'd go on break, find a nice piece of grass and walk in it, or better yet, sit on it, pressing my root chakra (my butt) to the earth and imagining my energy plugging into the Earth's energy. This would calm me right down. Everything would slow down; my thoughts, my breathing, my struggle.

Or I'd go hug one of those massive trees.... imagining its roots reaching deep into the Earth. They got a lot of hugging and a lot of me sitting against them, melding my energetic spine into their sturdy trunks. It was my safe-haven. My place of power. So calming.

This grove still exists, and Dan currently works in that building, oddly enough. So, there are times that I'll take him lunch and then go sit with the trees. I thank them for all the hugs they gave me so many years ago. It's like saying 'hi' to a group of old friends.

Even recently, I had something happen that caused a major emotional upheaval. I was trying to find a safe place to get my emotions under control and just couldn't find that place. I looked outside and there was a large rock next to a couple of trees. I went out, sat on the rock and it was like this solid hug from an old friend. I literally felt connected to the ground and watched over and protected by the trees. It took about 20 minutes, but I was able to then get up and deal with the situation calmer than I had started with.

There are sometimes that I can't get outside though. If I can't get outside, I go sit somewhere by myself and use my imagination to picture myself outside or plugging in through the floor of whatever building I'm in. It removes me from the situation, calms me down and allows me to bring the logic back into play.

It's very valuable for those of us that may go through triggers or other kinds of emotional upheavals, and it's so simple.

It's amazing how doing something so minor can be so powerful. I've become an intimate friend with this tool and have taken many hikes in the woods and hugged many trees over the years.

Dan says...

So, I don't really do much with chakras or medians or any of that cool stuff. It is a very experiential thing and I would not argue your experience – but I recognize that I don't normally connect to energy in that way.

I do connect to grounding, though. Regardless of the 'how it works', it does work, at least for me. When I am feeling intense emotions, it can be valuable to just sit and breath, visualizing the breath entering and leaving the nose, then the throat, then the lungs, and then the belly. I find that this simple practice tends to clear out of control emotions. It doesn't fix anything or erase anger/tension/fear, but it does slow it down enough that my rational brain gets involved as well.

TOOL #24 –
MEDITATION

Dan says...

I've noticed in some of our more "challenging" conversations that something comes out of my mouth that is not only untrue, but simply not what we are actually discussing - instead I dredge up past events; other times I am reacting on fear of the future when I really don't have a clue of what the future will bring.

Although meditation isn't a tool normally taught in polyamory classes, it certainly should be. It has been a strong and powerful way to help me with a variety of poly thought processes (and outside of poly as well). Simply put, meditation will bring you to being present in whatever is going on. Instead of being stuck in the past or the future, or borrowing trouble that doesn't exist, or replaying those old tapes regardless of the players being different, meditation helps us gain insight to our actual current situation. It need not be a religious or spiritual practice; it is a practical tool for being in the here and now

You might think that you can't meditate because you can't sit in a lotus position or you don't have time to go off to a three-day retreat. but none of those are needed. Meditation is as simple as sitting down and breathing - there really isn't much more to it. I'll explain it a bit more, because people like to have a playbook or a guide book to check in with sometimes, but really, it isn't at all complicated.

The benefits - in my life, in my partner's life - have been huge, but don't take my word for it - feel free to stop and Google 'meditation and stress', 'meditation and post-traumatic stress disorder', or even 'meditation and Google'.

Let's get down to it then. Here is a simple guide to learn how to meditate.

Sit
You can use a meditation cushion (zafu) or meditation bench (Seiza Bench) or just use a chair. If using a chair (which I often do), make sure it is a solid one (no desk chairs with wheels). Sit toward the front edge of your chair. Once you are sitting, you'll want to roll your pelvis forward, so you are sitting on the two bones in

your bottom, sometimes called the sitting bones. Allow your back to be straight and dip your chin a bit. In your sitting, find a balance. You don't want to be worried about being sitting ramrod straight, but don't slouch either. Think of the string of a musical instrument - not too tight or too loose.

Breathe

Rest attention on the breath as it travels in and out of the nose and allow yourself to feel the breath. You may find it useful to count it - on the in breath, mentally say "in", and on the outbreath, mentally count "one". We will come back to the breath in a minute.

Hands. Do something with your hands. You may want to make a steeple, or "lions' paw", or forefinger and thumb touching, or prayer hands, or something else. Regardless of which position (mudra) you pick, it is yours, and you'll want to keep using it when you meditate.

Mind

Here is the part that people find the most challenging, both in getting over their own preconceived views of what meditation is as well as what they are supposed to be doing...and just sitting still with yourself! As you sit and breathe, with the intent to rest attention on the breath, counting away, you'll find the mind wants to wander. Stories of the past, the future, what else you could be doing, are you doing this right, I took a right on my way to work when I meant to go left but I came across a nice little store where I found that vase that had... oh right, meditating. Your mind will wander. It is ok. If your mind wanders 10,000 times during your sitting, it is ok. Come back to the breath. I use a mantra I heard that, as I recognize my mind has wandered, I say to myself "Recognize, relax, return to the breath". I am acknowledging that my mind has wandered, I am not allowing myself to be frustrated about it, and I am getting back to sitting with the breath.

Simplify

- One thing that will make this practice easier is to be consistent in when and where you meditate (every morning, by this bookcase)
- Start with a timer set for 10 minutes. When you are ready, you may find it beneficial to go to 20 or 30 minutes.
- If you find yourself saying "I am not doing a good job at meditation!" then congratulate yourself on your sitting in one spot for 10 minutes of practice.
- When meditation is easy, then practice meditation when it is easy. When meditation is hard, practice meditation when it is hard.

Dawn says...

Meditation is truly the main tool I will recommend to someone when they ask how to tone down their PTSD symptoms or moments of emotional upheaval. Meditation teaches us mindfulness and how to be present in the moment and it's by being present that we'll be able to handle most of our emotional issues or not let our emotions get out of hand.

Meditation teaches our brain to concentrate on the moment. It teaches us to breathe and relax. It teaches us to let go of the stories that our brain seems determined to fill our head with.

Through the practice of sitting for 20 minutes a day, I've learned how to come back to the present, even when I've been triggered. Triggers that used to last for weeks, sometimes I can begin to control them almost instantly by letting go of the attached story to whatever emotion is going on.

Each morning, I sit for 20 minutes, either on my pillow in front of my altar in our meditation room, or in a chair wherever I may be, including the hotel we are in today. I light a candle for a focal point, which I need sometimes. I set the timer so that I don't have to keep looking at the clock, place my hands in a certain position so that I queue my body that we are going to meditate, take a deep breath and close my eyes most of the way.

For me, I don't close my eyes all the way because I will get lost in stories or I'll detach and float away. That's not the purpose of this mindful meditation. Instead, my goal is to stay present in that room.

I'm training my mind to be present and, in the moment, not drifting off somewhere. That's a different type of meditation. With this type of meditation, if my mind floats off and I recognize I'm telling myself a story, I stop the story, congratulate myself on being present enough to recognize that I was in a story and then I come back to the breath. If another story starts, which it will, our minds are creative little things, I do the same thing again. Wash, rinse, repeat.

And if there are noises to work around, all the better! If I hear a clock ticking in the room I'm meditating in, great! That means I'm present. If I hear the traffic, again, great! I'm present and in the moment. When the cat scratches herself against my hands, I smile, give a thanks of gratitude, maybe give her a pet, enjoy being in the moment and then go back to breathing.

Later, when I'm not meditating, and my mind starts telling me a story or I get lost in an old tape or an old reaction or am experiencing fear of the future, I stop the story. I come back to the breath and let it go.

The more you meditate, the slower your mind will become so that you can think things through and stop the stories. Have a problem with being passive aggressive and you want to change this? Meditate. Have problems with self-esteem because of the stories you tell yourself? Meditate.

There are major studies going on with the benefit of meditation with PTSD, and depression and all sorts of issues. They are starting to find proof to validate what many of us have known for a long time.

TOOL #25 – SEE WHAT IS NOW

Dan says...

Often when a partner starts a new relationship I want to know "where it is going". Sometimes this is based on simple curiosity; other times because I want to be involved in my lover's life and share their joy at something new developing. Unfortunately, often I will ask because of fear of the unknown. If I can quantify the new relationship - label it or give it a timeline - it will reduce my unease. I want to know 'Is this a new play partner, occasional date, someone I will have to put on my birthday list...?' And 'where do you see this going?'.

After years of this, I have finally figured out we never actually know. Sometimes things start great and end after a few months. And sometimes what I think is a simple fun date turns into looking around years later and realizing we have a serious bond - often to the surprise of all involved.

So even if my partner says, "I think they will be around for about six months and mainly will be here for watching those Korean drama shows I like that you don't", then all this does is allow me to create a false sense of security. False, because the truth is that we never know how relationships will develop regardless of our intent.

Another way we try to understand new relationships - and thus control our fear and resistance to them - is by recognizing milestones. There is a well-known and often written concept of the relationship escalator, that is to say, the expectation that a romantic relationship should follow a set of predefined steps which lead from that first date, the first kiss, and eventually to marriage, parenthood, and so on. In polyamory, this doesn't need to work this way, but we get trapped into old thinking and end up that sometimes we've defined relationships by the milestones.

For example, as Dawn starts to date someone new, I'll ask her 'did you kiss after the date?'. If yes, I set that in my head and wonder about the next one - have you had sex, intercourse, holding hands? Then the emotional ones as well - do you talk daily, say I love you, and finally say in love with you? Each one makes me adjust in my head how 'serious' the relationship is and kicks in a feeling of 'oh boy they are planning an overnight, Dawn only does that with people she really, really likes'.

Part of our solution is simply to admit we really don't know. Emotions are whacky and fluid and not willing to be held on a track. We might think the next relationship is The Big Love and it fades quickly, or we might find an FWB is suddenly making our heart pitter-patter, so, don't worry about it. I know that sounds simplistic, but in truth, when we recognize we don't know the future of a situation, we can instead be aware of how we feel today and focus on that.

After guessing about where a relationship - either mine or a partner's - is going, we started to use a tool we call 'See What Is Now'. Although you might have seen this tool in Corporate America or a Zen class, the idea is the same - the future is unknown and the more time I spend in 'what if' fantasies, the more my discomfort grows.

There is nothing wrong with the curiosity of wondering what my partner sees in a new person or where they think it might be going, but it is often a great opportunity to reframe the question from 'where is the relationship going?' to 'why do I have fear and resistance to new people?'. This leads me to an even better question, 'what can I do about my fear and resistance?'.

Dawn says...

So, what is this concept of 'See what is Now'' – what does that mean? Basically, it means to 'live in the moment'. Many of us are wrapped up in things that have happened in the past or worry about what may happen in the future, instead, try to remember to enjoy now.

Breathe, and as our mind wanders and gets stuck in a loop of fear or worry or even remembrance of another time, bring your focus back to the truth of what is happening right now. If we get caught up in the past or future, basically, we are shitting on the moment. We will never get this moment back, so why spend it thinking about other things?

When I'm with a partner and I'm worried about the future or worried about anything really, it doesn't even have to be about them or us, it could be something completely different. Regardless, I try to bring my thoughts back to the moment. I take a breath and blink my eyes and feel something solid that I'm touching. That grounds me (this is talked about in another part of the book) and brings me back to the present. Meditation really helps with this. It slows the mind down so that you can bring your focus back to what is important, the present moment.

Whatever happened in the past, happened. It's done. And whatever is going to happen it the future hasn't happened yet. So, really be present. Today, now, right this moment, is the only time this moment will happen. Make the most of it by being aware of it and present for it.

Now, I also realize that not all 'now's' are enjoyable places to be. So, if it's not, you don't have to enjoy it, but at least 'experience now' for what it is.

One way of slowing the mind and thoughts down enough so that you can wrangle them, bring them under control and be in the now so that you can enjoy it or experience it, is through meditation – another tool we talked about.

AND MORE...

The following chapters are experiences that don't fit in the previous tools section as they don't point at one specific tool. Yet, they are reflections on our nearly two decades of practicing polyamory; from specifics tips around polyamory flirting and learning compersion, to reflections on when you have to leave one partner out of something, to dealing with being an abuse survivor, or simply the cross section of polyamory and Leather, or power exchange, or geekiness. We believe that you might see yourself or your situations in these chapters and hope you find value in them.

IT'S NOT ALWAYS
JEALOUSY

Dawn says...

Many of our poly tools have to do with how to help us with jealousy.... but sometimes it's not jealousy that we may need help with, instead, it's our own feelings of self-worth, self-confidence or having to work on baggage that is brought up from a new relationship - any new relationship - one's we've started, or a partner has started.

We usually dump all these negative emotions under the 'jealousy' category. But, if we do that, are we causing a disservice to ourselves and our personal growth? 'Oh, it's just jealousy', but there is more to look at.

When we are in a monogamous relationship, it's easier to hide some of our 'character flaws'...or for that matter, to not even realize we have any 'character flaws' to work on. If we have a lack of something about ourselves, it's easy to work around it without ever knowing what 'it' is. But, add new relationships into the mix and things bubble (or for some of us, explode) to the surface, because we must look in the mirror if something has happened that has made us miserable. If there is suffering involved, which sometimes happens, we must look at ourselves and what is causing it. Before we blame others' actions, we really need to look at ourselves, or these feelings will constantly crop up.

Have an issue with rejection? Easy enough to hide in a monogamous relationship. It can show up as jealousy when you see your partner looking at someone else a little too long or when they are talking to someone at work. It's not jealousy though; not all the time. It's a fear of rejection or abandonment, but in a monogamous relationship we fix it by asking or telling our partner not to do it again, because it's their fault you feel this way. Bam. Problem solved. You can blame it on someone else and never have to self-reflect on what just caused those emotions.

But, with polyamory, there are so many things that will happen that cause this emotion to rear its head. Each time a new relationship is started, or when something new is attempted with each new partner. So many things can cause these emotions;

an unexpected text at an odd time, something out of place after a date and again we dump them all under jealousy, which really is a way to just hide the true emotion. You need to find out what the true emotion is and work on that or your poly life is going to involve a lot of suffering for everyone involved.

Are you feeling a lack of self-confidence? Not uncommon. Do you set up rules in your relationships so that these emotions don't arise, or do you admit this is the emotion and work on your lack of self-confidence? Or a little of both? For me, I recognized what was going on (after a long struggle with this intense feeling) and asked for some rules to be put into place while I worked on myself. These rules were placed with intent, and it was comforting when I would hear my partner, "Dawn is having an issue with rejection, so I'm going to help her out by not doing this one thing that seems to trip her up, while she is working on herself." But, then, I had to do the work.

This helped a lot and helped me learn the trust involved to build self-confidence; both the trust in my partner and the more importantly, the trust in myself. Then, as my confidence grew, we were able to get rid of most of the "rules." Sometimes our journey involved baby steps, but by setting that intention to work on myself and asking for my partners' assistance at times, I've been able to smooth out many of these emotions.

And then, what if it's not something I've mentioned above, but more 'territorial'? Ouch.

Some people are a little more self-aware in current times and have already done some research on this topic or have the idea that they aren't an 'owned' person and don't have the right to 'own' anyone else.

Some of us were brought up differently and it's taken time to realize that we are still working in this mode with our relationships. I was absolutely working in this mode without realizing it and it caused a lot of pain at the beginning of us dating separately. I had to do a lot of work in a lot of ways to get through this.

But I was reminded of it while watching 'Ginger the Poly Puppy' one morning. You see, 'Ginger the Poly Puppy' isn't so poly some days. She likes to have a lot of humans in her life, but she doesn't always like to share her humans, and when it comes to her territory with the cat.... she doesn't share well at all.

It reminded me as I'm watching the dog guard her water bowl from the cat this morning, that not all issues with poly are jealousy.

I'm watching a battle between cat and dog over territory. 'Mine' is what the dog is saying. 'This is my water that mom just filled up for me'....'this is my space that was created for me', and when the cat dips her paw into the water as if to say 'really? you think this is just yours, let me show you that it isn't just yours' and continues to dip her paw into the water until the dog chases her away.

In the past, when I've asked monogamous people why they are monogamous, occasionally the response is 'I'm too territorial to share', and I totally get that. Humans can be pretty primal with primal instincts. Sometimes we think of ourselves as enlightened beings, but we also have lizard brains. Maybe that's where our territorial feelings come from?

So, that feeling doesn't have to be jealousy.... it's not a 'I want what they have'. Instead, it's territorial, 'you are not having what's mine'. And sometimes we aren't talking about people. What if it's an environment that you've created for yourself?

For example, my relationship with Dan. I've put a LOT of work into that. Lots of work, lots of designing our 'perfect' relationship. Our dream relationship. Our fantasy. Then, someone else comes in. It's not Dan that I own, but it's the relationship that I feel is mine that I created that someone else is stepping into and changing. Someone is changing my secure environment that I finally have in my life, that I never had before. I never felt safe. And now someone is coming in that I haven't vetted as a safe person. Unfortunately, it takes me a LONG time to feel safe with anyone. I knew Dan for 14 years before we started this relationship. And this person is changing my environment, my territory....and there isn't anything I can do about it. Each time a new person comes in, I must re-create my safe environment and it's a lot of work.

And yet, we are poly, this is what we do. We invite people in to share our lives, or they invite us in to share theirs.

It would be nice if I didn't need a safe environment, and I'm not as clingy to that concept as I used to be, but when you come from a childhood environment that was never safe, safety is very important to me. Trusting the new people not to drink from my water bowl because they feel they have the right to, regardless of the fact that it's stepping on 'my' space......feels rude and invasive. Ok, I know I tell the dog to share with the cat, but some days I can see it clearly through the dog's point of view.

It would be nice if I could get the dog to be gracious with her water bowl. 'See, mommy got me clean water and I'd like to share it with you...I know she'll get me more later.'

It would be nice if I could get to the point of, 'see the safe environment I created with this loving, gracious man? I'd like to share it with you and anyone he wants to bring in. I know he'll be there for me as well, and while loving other people.'

It's hard to teach a pup to share and be gracious and not so territorial, we humans get a chance to realize what is going on and decide if we want to be territorial or open our arms, lives and homes to others with love.

Dan says...

In my monogamous relationships, if I got jealous, it was easy to fix. My partner should stop doing anything that will make me jealous.

This type of thinking was not actually fixing jealousy, or anything else. It would hide things for a time, but in reality, I made an error (that I believe is pretty common) - I expected that when I didn't like something in the relationship, my partner would change so that it would no longer be an issue. If I was doing something to make them unhappy...well, I needed to either give it up or hide better.

This is not really a great attitude regarding jealousy (or any other aspect of relationships) but it is how many of us are taught things work. But it doesn't' work - either for monogamy or, perhaps more so, in polyamory. I'm not saying that I don't speak up and ask my partners for adjustments - 'please don't leave your socks on the floor' or 'if you have a date, remember to put it on the calendar' are just part of being a partnership. But a lot of the time me being uncomfortable or unhappy requires me to fix me, not expecting someone else to do the work or to stop doing behaviors that make me look at myself.

Or said in another way, I can't both tell my partner "let's be polyamorous" and "don't do anything to make me jealous". I do say 'help me with my feelings' (we address how to ask your partner for help elsewhere in this book).

So, when I believe that jealousy is rising, here are some of the steps I take to evaluate jealousy...and to determine if it is jealousy or something else.

First of all, I made a distinction between jealousy ("I don't want you to have this") and envy ("I want what you're having!"). Often, this distinction can take the fight out of jealousy and help give me a clear path to what I need.

Envy is easier for me to reframe as an 'ok' emotion that can be as simple as 'I'm upset that my partner took someone to a favorite bar; I want to go to that bar as well. I will ask my partner to take me...or I will go by myself. Or....

And my partner would have a clear way to assist me - often by making sure I get some of (whatever it is) as well.

Next, I realize that sometimes jealousy isn't anything other than keeping score. My partner has another date and I don't, and I feel sad and deprived. If I do happen to realize this, it can help to instead focus on excitement for my partner. As I discuss elsewhere in the book, try to practice an attitude of generosity and graciousness. Plus, I try to change my outlook to looking forward to time on my own - either riding my bike on rambling tours, or reading in a coffee shop, or my other hobbies. Sometimes when I hear my partner has a date, I secretly think "woohoo, alone time!". Recently, I simply said it out loud - lucky for me they recognize I am an introvert.

Much to my annoyance, sometimes jealousy is actually a feeling of entitlement. They are getting more sex, more love, more time together, more attention, etc. Once more, a great counter for this is to actively practice generosity and graciousness.

Additionally, once recognized, I make it a habit of sitting with that feeling of entitlement. What does that feel like, entitlement? Why do I deserve more? Do I want my partner to be who they are, or should they only be what I want them to be? It doesn't take long for me to realize that it is not only ignoble, but just plain selfish. That's not who I want to be.

HOW TO LEARN
COMPERSION

Dan says...

One of the harsher comments I've heard in regard to dealing with jealousy and envy at a polyamory discussion group was "You choose to feel a lack of compersion; you'll never get polyamory".

Although I know some people who felt compersion was second nature to them, most people I've met had to learn that relationship sharing doesn't mean a lack of love. That is what was modelled for me - by the media, by my peers. So, the idea that my wife is holding another man's hand (or cock) is something that has taken time to process. For me, compersion comes and goes. I can be centered and full of joy for my partner's joy one day and the next grumpy that they are on "another date doing fun stuff and probably forgot about me..."

So how do you learn compersion? First, realize you already know what compersion is - joy in another's joy - and you likely experienced it as well - at least in general. A child's happiness at a favorite TV show you don't personally care about; a good friend getting a promotion, or when your partner finds the perfect shoes - you might not care about shoes, but you are happy they are happy. This is the same feeling. It just feels different because there is an aspect of polyamory compersion that says "If they have happiness with someone else, what about me? Am I still part of this picture?"

So, since you know what it is, how do you make it part of your life? How do you cultivate this emotion to be a natural part of you?

For me, I've found the solution is to create situations that allow compersion to arise more easily. In other parts of this book, Dawn and I have talked about "the Why", that foundation of why you are exploring polyamory, and this is a big part of how you can invite compersion into your life. When you can recognize, at least at a mental or logical level, that when you feel jealous or possessive that the situation is not only ok, but clearly part of who you are, that is a first step.

Next, I have certainly found that I do much better with compersion when my needs are being met. If I am already fulfilled sexually, feeling secure in our relationship emotionally, and might even be thinking "I sure love my partner, but it would be nice to chill alone with a video game tonight" then compersion comes pretty easy. So, I keep in mind that the opposite is true - it can be hard to be happy for others when I am unhappy, either unhappy with a partner, or even just generally. So, practice what brings you joy outside of your relationships - hobbies and passions, spending time with non-romantic friends, or a PlayStation marathon, whatever is fun for you when you put you first - be it a solo motorcycle ride or a night of board games with platonic pals.

These, as well as other tools in this book, end up with a cumulative impact to bring compersion closer to the surface and make it more likely to be my reaction. And even when it is not the immediate reaction, it still gets there. Sometimes I must breathe, take a step back, and ask myself 'How am I responding? How do I want to respond? I need to step up and recognize that I can do better'.

Dawn says...

Compersion has been a hard one for me. I truly want to feel it, for both my partners and my metamours, but for some of us, it's easy logically, not so much emotionally.

Over 20 years, I've only met 2 people that have shared with me that they have never felt jealousy. Everything is about compersion and the other person's happiness. I believed them and thought they were super lucky. Actually, I was envious. Life must be so much easier that way. Then, one day, one of them came to me, all stressed out and started explaining this emotion of fear and feeling left out and that feeling of dread in the pit of his stomach and he wanted to keep her home. He didn't want her having fun with this new person. I had to sit him down and tell him that a lot of people call that jealousy. He was floored. Over the many years he'd been living this lifestyle and after the many partners he had had, he'd never experienced this feeling.

We sat for a while and started pulling the pieces apart, because there can be a lot of things layered under the umbrella term of jealousy. We figured out that he wasn't as confident in this particular relationship as he had been with the others he'd been involved in and that lead to these feelings. So, to get back onto the track of compersion, he decided to work on his confidence with their relationship. He also added in meditation so that he could slow his mind down a little.

Over time, he was able to balance himself and get back to his normal way of relating and experiencing happiness for his partner.

For him, his normal mode of relating was through compersion. For many of us, we must learn it or, re-learn.

A little more about me...

I knew I was polyamorous before polyamory was a word; it was a concept that just felt right. I had a boyfriend in high school that I'd met at church camp of all places. We lived in different counties and didn't get to see each other unless I snuck out of the house and drove to meet him. After months of dating, I had a friend tell me that she had seen him with someone else. I shrugged my shoulders. It wasn't a surprise. We went to different high schools and he was a little younger than me. Why wouldn't he date others? It made perfect sense to me.

I would have preferred he told me about them himself, instead of hiding it, but that's what we were taught. And when I told him this, he didn't believe that I was ok with it. Hell, I wanted to meet his other girlfriend to see what she was like. That went over like a ton of bricks. Why would he believe I had well-meaning intentions? He assumed I was jealous and was trying to get close to her to damage his and her relationship. I mean, that's what they do on TV, right?

Then, my friends got involved. They considered it their duty to convince me that I was being a doormat and allowing him to walk all over me just to keep him. I looked at it and started questioning myself. As a survivor, was I letting him use me? Maybe I was. So, I started calling him out on it, which took him by surprise since I had convinced him I was ok with him dating others. Needless to say, I had become the person that he had assumed I was to begin with and now he couldn't trust me. That relationship didn't last much longer. It was a shame because it was really good until 'friends' convinced me I was doing it wrong. Then, their way of thinking became ingrained and I've struggled getting back to my original way of relating. I'm much better at it now that I'm using all these tools though.

AGREEMENTS

Dan says...

When Dawn and I started to explore polyamory as a couple, we, like many people that approach polyamory from an existing couple perspective, set up some rules. Rules that seemed to be 'no brainers', such as "condoms are mandatory", were easy to accept. We had other rules that we viewed as ways to express respect for each other, such as "partner gets to meet the new person before intimacy occurs". Other rules we discussed that were each problematic in their own way included 'no one comes in the home', 'other partners can't come to your work', 'no open mouth kissing', 'no falling in love' and 'the veto rule' (more about those last two in a few moments).

Within the polyamory community in general, rules are viewed with a wide spectrum of response, some positive, some negative (and some extremely 'don't try to control me' negative). We didn't understand the negative view at first, as on the surface, our rules were intended to help us navigate communication and expectations. But we realized later that often rules can be about trying to create a sense of personal and relationship safety – an unconscious idea that if we have walls around our behavior and a set of clearly defined 'what is allowed/not allowed', we would be more 'in control' and thus, things would be less scary.

The problem with rules is that, when they are not upheld to an assumed standard or not understood the same way by both people, it can cause resentment, lack of trust, and a feeling of being lied to. For example, "condoms are mandatory". We thought here is an easy, simple rule that makes sense. But condoms imply a penis, so what about girl/girl sex? What about oral sex? Whatever your answer might be, don't just say 'well the answer to that is common knowledge'. Dawn and I thought the same...but had a different understanding of what that common knowledge was!

So, our approach to rules has changed over the years. I try to keep in mind that if a partner wants to introduce rules into our poly to have empathy for them – they are most likely trying to find security in a situation where they perceive they have none and the rules are a way to mitigate that fear. I then ask myself, "how do you feel about each one?". Does it seem reasonable to me? I look at each one, decide how it feels, and if I disagree with it, I keep my partner as a partner and have them help us find a compromise.

But overall, I ask my partner to reframe rules to agreements. Meaning, instead of a rule that says 'never get a girl's phone number without consulting me first', an agreement that says 'if you believe you are engaging with a new girl and it gets to the point that you are going to get her phone number, let me know about that as soon as you can'. This represents a desire to be informed as you make new connections. Versus the rule, which could be interpreted as 'I want to control who you can/can't talk to'.

One more tricky bit about rules is who all must agree to them? For example, between Dawn and me and Karen, we are all fluid bonded, and we share a common agreement that 'sex with people outside of our circle must include protection – meaning condoms for penetration and oral sex, or in the case of girls, dental dams'. As our fluid bonded circle grew to include Dawn's boyfriend, then he must understand that we had that rule. And that if he did not follow it, then we needed to know that - then either I or Karen might decide not to be fluid bonded with the group anymore.

As I mentioned before, I want to talk a bit more about two common poly rules, 'no falling in love' and 'veto power'.

The 'No Falling in Love' Rule

Unfortunately, this is simply a bad rule for poly folk. You might say "I'm ok with my partner dating, having sex, and loving others, but I don't want them to FALL in love with them". The reason this rule is bad is because it might not be able to be kept. I have never fallen in love with someone with any purpose, or not loved someone due to a decision. Love happens. Don't set up a rule that will give you an illusion of something that your partner can't control.

The 'Veto' Rule

The veto rule is simply an agreement between two (or more) partners that one partner can say 'No' to an additional relationship, regardless of explanation or discussion, and that the other relationship will then end. It is normally thought of as impacting new relationships but that should be clarified as well.

This is a hot topic for many polyamory communities.

Some explanations that people shared of why they find it of value include...

• "Right now, my partner has veto power if he feels that someone I'm seeing/considering playing with poses a risk to our sexual health and refuses to practice safer sex (or tries to convince me not to)".

- "Its presence is important though, because it offers a feeling of control during times when I feel like there is none. After a difficult conversation about changes or problems, for example, I might say something like 'Hey, if I really needed all of this to end, it would, right?' And then he says of course, and we continue. But like, I've never really been tempted to use it, mostly because that would mean that my and his wishes were different to the point that we couldn't compromise, which hasn't happened yet. Unless he was really making a dumb move that he didn't understand, I don't think I'd want to set a precedent in the relationship that things can be so easily dropped. But the sentiment is important to me, for sure".

- "That's the arrangement my wife and I have, we both have veto over each other's 'other'. So far, we haven't had to use it. But yeah if there ever was someone who was a problem each of us is here to act as a sanity check for the other".

On the other hand, some people dislike it, even see it as destructive.

- "I was dating a man whose wife had veto power and though she technically never used it with regards to me, she did hold it over my head, and as a result, I never trusted her. Her having this power and having extensive control over aspects of my relationship with her husband that I just do not agree with on a fundamental level meant that she and I could never have a good or healthy relationship with each other. I always had the sense that if I did something that she didn't like, she'd either threaten to veto me or actually veto me. In my mind, that's just not good poly".

- "It made me feel insecure and disposable. It made me need more reassurance and such than I otherwise would have".

- "People can re-negotiate their relationships with me, but they can't negotiate my relationships with other people!"

I wanted to give you that background before sharing our view. To be honest, I have a hard time answering the question "Is the veto rule good or bad?". Instead of answering that, I would advise that you avoid the whole mess and find an alternative that accomplishes the same basic idea - helping you feel confident in the relationship you have as you seek to open it up.

So, some alternatives to the Veto Rule! How about an agreement with our partner(s) that if there is something that someone is doing that feels disrespectful or unhealthy, we get to voice it, and in turn, the other listens. And yes, set time aside and really listen. We recognize that sometimes that's hard, especially during NRE, but part of the commitment is the promise that we will try our best. Don't worry about if the partner is "right" or "wrong", just listen and hear. Remember that they are sharing their feelings, their perception of facts. You may think that a new love is great and wonderful and yet a partner might say they are mean and spiteful. Is the partner just jealous? Or do they see something you don't see? Let your partner have a voice and find out what you can do to be a partner – how can you help your partner with what they are feeling.

Now, this might seem like a far cry from the Veto rule, but unless you are in a power exchange relationship (addressed elsewhere in this book) it might be best to avoid making demands of your partners, at best, it leads to resentment.

Our experience is that they can be both beneficial as well as problematic, but the better method is to skip rules and instead develop agreements.

Dawn says...

I am finally in a relationship where I feel safe, protected and loved. As a trauma survivor, that is very important to me. So, when we first started our journey into polyamory, we did have rules and we both had veto power. It was a way to feel secure in our current relationship and be able to connect to others. Healthy? Not? Don't know. But it's what we did, and it worked. Over time we shifted those 'rules' as we grew until we didn't need them anymore, to feel safe with ourselves, regardless of our or other relationships.

Sometimes, this can take a lot of work on the self to get where you are confident enough to handle most situations, to feel your jealousy and use it as a tool for growth. You don't need so many structures in place to feel in control.

At this point, we have agreements on how to communicate and I have different agreements with different partners, depending on what is important in that relationship and what kind of communication works best for each relationship. And we are aware that these agreements may change. Personally, I believe if any of the agreements are built out of fear, over time they should change, as we become more confident as people.

CAN WE GO BACK TO
BEING MONO?

Dan says...

Once you've opened the door and walked into polyamory, can you ever go back? I've tried it on occasion but never really with conviction. Only as a reaction to a bad time - "Fine, we will just not see other people, and I won't have to deal with my (jealousy/fear/lack of trust/etc.)". But it doesn't stick, at least not for me. For me, being polyamorous is a core aspect of who I am, and once I tasted it, once I've realized that I can love more than one person and that we (a large poly community) are out there, and I am not just weird but instead just wired different than monogamous people, then there is no chance of long term happiness if I deny this aspect of who I am. Loving more than one, sharing myself, being able to be open to new relationships if they come my way, tasting all of life without the limitations of a monogamous society, this is who I am. Facing everything that makes polyamory hard is part of who I am as well, and growing from it, and having partners that support my struggles.

Dawn says...

For me, once I allowed myself to embrace my polyamorous nature, I really don't think I could go back to being monogamous. Sometimes, I try to picture Dan coming home and saying, "Honey, I want to go back to living as a monogamous couple." And though I love him a lot, and we are very happy together, I just can't imagine living that monogamous lifestyle again. The idea of giving up the other relationships that I have, well the idea of it hurts, or the idea of giving up ANY chance of having another relationship, feels wrong to me.

Now, that's just my feelings on it. There are also people that aren't particularly 'wired' polyamorous and could live either lifestyle depending on the situation they are in. They may even prefer the poly lifestyle, but it's not something that is inherently part of their make-up nor a NEED that they have. So, for them, I've seen people of this nature flip back and forth with no real problems. It's just another way to do relationships.

Personally, I NEED the opportunity to have multiple relationships; I NEED all my partners to be ok with this. If I don't have this, I can guarantee that I'll cheat again and that's not the life I want to live, nor the partnership that I want to offer someone.

NO RIGHT WAY

Dawn says...

Over the years, many people have asked us what is the 'right way' to do polyamory. We don't have a specific relationship style that we would recommend. There are so many ways you can do this, and no 2 relationships are the same. There is mono/poly, solo poly, coamory, don't ask don't tell, poly pods, poly families, poly tribes, kitchen table poly, parallel poly and really, too many to mention and some styles that don't have a name.

Basically, what I tell people is to do what works for you and don't let anyone try to put you in a box or tell you what is right and wrong. Be honest with yourself, be honest with your partners, set your boundaries, know your truth, be open to love and connection. If you need to work on your baggage, work on your baggage. If you find yourself becoming jealous, use that as a tool for learning about yourself and finding the tools that are needed for your growth as a person.

Find the polyamory style that works for you. This could be different with each relationship you are involved in. And each relationship could shift over time. Go with the flow and if you are being ethical (how you and your partners define it, not how 'they' define it), polyamory can be done many, many ways.

Dan says...

When someone asks me what kind of polyamory I practice, I often say Chaos Hybrid. If they nod knowingly like a polyamory expert, I smile to myself – I made that term up. If instead, they say "Oh? What is that?", it gives us a place to start talking. But if I was trying to come up with an honest answer to it, I'd say "I practice a polyamory based on tools that I've found effective so far which balances between the needs of the one and the needs of the relationships and realize that it may change tomorrow and I'll do my best to flow with it" style...so maybe Chaos Hybrid is a pretty good title for it after all.

MISSING ONE PARTNER WHEN YOU ARE WITH ANOTHER

Dawn says...

I'm imagining I'm not the only one that goes through this.... the confusion of missing one partner when I'm with another.

One time, I left to go to the boyfriends, and knew I was going to miss Dan. But I'd also been missing my boyfriend and wanted to go spend time with him. We hadn't had any alone time in a while. At the same time, I also knew that the boyfriend would be missing his wife, who was away on a trip. I'm sure she missed her husband and her boyfriend, as well.

It's such a conundrum and for me, one of the hard things of doing a long-distance relationship. There isn't much option to have all of us together so that I can be with them both at the same time. I can't do like Dan did, and move his other partner in with us. Well, she didn't exactly move in with us.... the 3 of us bought a house together. But, he's able to go to either side of the house and visit either of us at any time. I can't do that. I must leave Dan to visit Raymond.

I do get to be with both, and sometimes all 3 of them when we are tabletop gaming. It's fun, but we are gaming. It's different.

Another time, there was a Sunday morning, as I'm sitting on Raymond's patio, enjoying the breeze and the company, I didn't want to go home. Though, it's not that I don't want to go home, it's that I don't want to leave where I'm at. Then, when I come home, I'm excited to see Dan, but I am missing Raymond.

I do stay in contact with Raymond when I'm home, and I stay in contact with the husband when I'm with the boyfriend. Just like each of them stays in contact with their other partners when they are with me. Any other way and I feel that I'd be separating people we love from people they love. (I was going to say 'of course' at the beginning of this paragraph, but then realized not everyone does their poly this way).

There isn't a 'fix' for this situation. It is what it is. Neither of us will be moving as we each own a house and have kids, and jobs; so, the distance is there. The missing of them is there. I guess it shows how much I enjoy their company and love being with them. I thought it would get easier, but so far, it's still a challenge.

What tools do I use for this? I don't think I have anything specific.... except not dwell on it because dwelling on it causes suffering. It was just a thought tonight as I sat down to write; next to Dan, while texting Raymond goodnight, getting ready to jump in the hot tub with Dan and Karen.

Dan says...

"I miss you" can be said as an endearment, as a statement of information, or even at times as a compliment. It is a bittersweet thing, part of loving someone and not being around them and it is ok to miss someone. It can cause a problem when we confuse missing someone to clinging.

It is fine to miss our lover when they are not around, but when we only miss them when they are with another partner, then we should look at ourselves and wonder if it is simply a recognition that we like it when they are around and it feels nice to be in their presence...or is it actually envy we feel, wishing we had what someone else has at that moment.

JUMPING OFF THE ESCALATOR

Dawn says...

One of the interesting things I've learned since being in poly relationships, is that there is a relationship escalator, and not all relationships have to ride one. I mean, when I was young and had just started dating, you were only to date people that were good marriage material. That's what my mother convinced me of anyway. Yes, I'm from an older generation, but you didn't date for fun. You jumped on the escalator and as soon as you dated for a little while, people started asking when you were going to get married. That's the relationship escalator. It's the idea that all relationships have an end goal, usually marriage.

It's an idea that most of us are raised with even though that language isn't used or at least my mother's generation had that philosophy and she tried to pass it down to me. It's that idea of being married to someone for the rest of your life, 2 kids and a dog and a white picket fence.

I clearly remember, my mom telling me that she didn't like the guy I was dating during high school because he wouldn't make a good husband. I wasn't looking for a husband at the time, so it didn't make any sense to me that I should be looking for those qualities in someone. He was fun, and I liked him. To me, that's all that mattered. But she was adamant that I should break up with him. I didn't. Well, not for those reasons anyway. Unfortunately, at that point she had drilled a bit into my head that I should only date prospective husbands. So, with the next boyfriend, I gave in and married him. He was a good guy, seemed like he'd be good with kids according to his family, and our other friends were getting married at the time and nagged us until we followed suit. It's what you did.

That marriage lasted a long time, but at some point, I just couldn't stay on that escalator. There was a chink in it, and it was jarring to stay on it. So, I jumped off and decided that there had to be other ways of doing relationships, ways I had thought of before as a teenager, with that high school boyfriend.

Now that I've had some experience living polyamorous, my idea of relationships has gone back to my original way of thinking; relationships don't have to lead to something permanent. There doesn't have to be an 'end goal'.

There doesn't have to be a wedding or a commitment ceremony. If it happens, it's fine, but it's not the goal when I start dating someone. Instead, I've gotten to where I'm ok being where I'm at in my relationships, regardless of where it is.

Each person is in my life, just the way they are. There may be 'next steps' involved...there might not be. For example, I may spend a certain amount of time with them before taking the next step of a sleepover. But, that's just because I'm a slow relationship builder. It doesn't mean that there is a plan in place to move any of my relationships to be any more than what they are now. I'm enjoying them for what they are.

Some may organically grow in a certain direction, but there isn't a guarantee, and I'm not just talking about current relationships but future ones as well. There isn't a 'meet, spend more time together, overnight, fluid bonded, commitment ceremony, move in' agenda. Again, it may happen, but that's not the goal.

Instead, it's realizing that these steps may never take place, and being ok with that. ...with Raymond, some of these steps were taken, but I don't ever see us moving in together, or some other top of the escalator moments.... but I'm good with that. If I was worried about the supposed 'end game', I wouldn't be enjoying what we have right now. I'd be stressing because we haven't moved to the 'next level' of the relationship, whatever that is supposed to be.

All my relationships are at different levels of intimacy and romance and sharing and commitment. That's the way I like it. That doesn't mean there isn't growth and nurturing in the relationships. It just means that they won't end with the white picket fence. Thank Goodness.

I know some people who will back out of a relationship if there isn't a promise of commitment somewhere or if they aren't riding the escalator at the same pace. I don't have that worry. I can be more relaxed.

And that is such a relief to figure out, otherwise I would be wondering what the next thing was that we had to accomplish to show our commitment towards each other. A weekend together? A week together? Fancy trips? ...or whatever else the escalator can look like.

Also, by not riding the escalator, there is less chance of me having expectations that are going to hurt me emotionally. If I'm enjoying the relationship for what it is and not comparing it to other relationships and not having an end goal in mind, that means that I'm not doubting our relationship and our feelings for each other. Riding the escalator isn't a sign of love. You can love each other and only see each other once a week, or be long distance, or whatever form the relationship takes. It is what it is.

It can get a little ugly if one partner is riding the escalator and the other isn't. I can remember dating a couple different girls in the past and when we first got together, I do what I usually do and showed them my calendar. I let them know what kind of time we had available and what our limitations were. I like people to be aware up front what they are getting into and what we have to offer, that we have no interest in moving anyone in. I didn't want them to be surprised later.

Each of them was excited and said they understood. I really thought they understood we had no end goal but moving in wasn't an option. I really thought the second one understood because we told her the story of the previous one. But, over time each of them started talking about when they'd be able to move in. We told them that wasn't going to happen. Both thought that when there was enough love, of course we'd want them to move in... because that's what you do in a relationship if you love someone. Sorry to say, those relationships didn't last because they took it personally that we weren't on the same escalator as them. They ended up hurt. We ended up hurt.

As a polyamorous person, jump off that escalator. We don't have to have an end game. Enjoy your relationships for what they are.

Dan says...

I have had a string of relationships that lasted six months. The thing is, I explain to people whom I start dating, I am busy right now, and although I want to date you and spend time with you, I really don't have a lot of extra time. I normally literally bring out my Google Calendar, so they can see what I am talking about. I explain that if we start dating, chances are we'll average seeing each other about a night a month. They say they get it, that it is fine and works great for them.

But it doesn't, and at about that six-month spot they say they need more, I explain I can't provide it, and they move on.

Sometimes we get thinking that all relationships need to be linear and moving from step to step - let's date, let's go steady, let's meet the parent, let's buy a house and have kids, etc. Polyamory doesn't follow that path. It can and might - but it might go another way, or stay like it is, or morph into something else, and it works best when you just let it happen.

It took me a long time to not try to fit relationships in a box - that is, to try to determine what a relationship is and what it is going to look like next week and the dreaded 'where are we going'. Now, things just are, and someone reminds me we've been dating for four years and I can happily smile and enjoy that place we are, wherever that is.

POLYAMOROUS FLIRTING

Dan says...

You've decided that you are polyamorous and although it is true you can identify as such even if you are single, it is more fun when you have partners! Finding people is one challenge; and once you found them, letting them know you are interested in them is the next. This section is to share some tips for flirting for polyamorous people.

Flirting is exciting and can lead to new romance and more. But let's take a moment to understand what flirting is - you'll find that it is a lot easier to be successful at flirting if your definition of success is the act of flirting itself. Meaning, in the bar scene, flirting might be 'getting someone to go home with me for sex'. In other situations, flirting might be to kick off a more linear process - first a date, then go steady, get engaged, then married. This is also known as the relationship escalator, but neither of these situations is what we are talking about. Instead, we want you to think about flirting as a present tense activity without the "and then" part. In other words, flirting for the sake of flirting itself, and if an email address is exchanged or a phone number and a promise to text happens, great, that is a bonus. We have found that when you approach things with this mindset, you have a much better chance at success; partly because you are more relaxed - you are not in it for high stakes - but also because you defined success as trying. This might be natural to you, or it might be way outside your comfort zone. These steps will help in either case!

Flirting Tips!

1 - Look approachable
- What should you wear? Something that makes it clear you are polyamorous, like a convention shirt from a polyamory convention, is one way to go about it. But the key factors are anything that is clean and simple. If it reflects you and your

personality, all the better. Also, a t-shirt with your favorite band or view of some issue can help as a conversation starter (we will take more about that in a moment).

- Regardless of what you were, relax and smile, and they can go hand in hand - the more you put a smile on your face, the more relaxed you'll tend to feel. Breathe.

2 - Learn some basic body language

- Do you look approachable? Are your arms folded and protective? Or are your arms and legs held casually, relaxed? Remember that confidence is sexy; so, reflect confidence. And how do you do that if you are not confident? Don't try to be confident, instead, practice being patient and mildly interested in everything. These two attributes will reflect someone who is present and ready for whatever to come along...and not concerned about what doesn't.

3 - Initiate conversation

- This is a hard one for lots of people but pay attention to the response. When you ask a question, do they respond? Is it a one-word response, or do they respond with their own question?
- Instead of asking about the weather (boring!), ask about the jewelry they are wearing, or a tattoo they have. Not "Is that a ring?" but "That ring looks special, is there a story behind it?" or "I love your ink; why did you decide that is a permanent part of your story?"
- Keep in mind though, when making conversation, speak to the person instead of the thing. For example, you have great teeth vs you have a beautiful smile
- Ask about other partners and respond with graciousness and generosity. Be happy that they have people in their lives if they do. Don't make it about you!
- Be a good listener. No, really, listen to the person. Give them time to talk. Don't get locked in on your own response.

4 - And then?

- And then...nothing. You are flirting. You are having a nice conversation. If you are done, say "I really enjoyed talking to you" and follow that up with smiling and walking away, or "I'd like to talk again if you are of a mind, can I give you my contact info?". Don't be attached to the answer - enjoy the conversation for its own sake. In the case you do want to share your personal info, we like to recommend simply business cards to hand out, even if it is just a name and email and phone, so you don't have to struggle for finding a pen and cocktail napkin.

Dawn says...

Flirting is a challenge for me. I am not a natural flirt like Dan. Also, I'm an introvert and I really don't like small talk. So, finding something to talk about can be challenging for me. I want to talk about deep topics, even topics that are taboo on a first date; politics and religion. I want to get to know the person on a deep level which usually intimidates some people. But, the people I'm currently in relationships with, we talked about heavy topics on the first date. I don't care about gossip and who is doing what and what the weather is.

So, if I'm on a date with someone new, I'll do what Dan suggested above. I'll either bring up something that piqued my interest from their profile if we are meeting from an online dating site, or I'll pick out a piece of jewelry or something like that to start a conversation. I also make sure to wear interesting jewelry to give them something to start a conversation with. Normally, I'll wear a ring or earrings with a polyamory symbol and/or I'll wear a chunky stone necklace that draws the eye. OK. if I'm really interested in flirting, I'll wear a shirt/blouse that shows a little cleavage and make sure the stone settles in the right spot. Whether they look, or how they look, can tell me a lot about that person.

Then, I try to remember to smile and watch them with a soft gaze. I'm not much of a smiler when I'm in conversation because I'm busy listening and concentrating. My memory sucks and I'm trying to remember details of what they are telling me as well as being in the present moment. But, if it's someone new, I try to remember to smile some so that they don't think I'm being judgmental, and they know I'm having a good time with them. I can be intense, or so I'm told. So, I try to tone it down a little. Unless, like with Raymond, I figure they can handle my intensity.

The other suggestion I would like to offer when flirting is to learn to have fun with it. It's a skill and does not come naturally for everyone. Don't have an end goal.... just practice, practice, practice, and it will start to flow naturally.

POLYAMORY SEX TIPS

Dan says...

Polyamory, like this book, is not about sex. But it is very true that many polyamory relationships include sex and sexuality, and this can be part of the challenge for many people regarding polyamory - with who (especially when it isn't "me"), when, why, even how often.

We included this chapter not so much as a 'sex guide' but instead think of it as a 'best practices around sex in a poly dynamic', because sharing deep intimate sexual connections with more than one person can indeed get tricky.

The first thing we recommend is talking to the people you are having sex with, and about who you are having sex with. Although some people prefer a 'don't ask, don't tell' policy, we believe you need to at least have a conversation about safer sex practices. And you'll need to be specific - do you require dental dams? Do you know what dental dams are?

Sometimes these conversations - especially if you are just getting started in polyamory - can be emotionally charged. I've found the best conversations have happened when we can sit in a place of calm and have back and forth conversations. My current partners don't want a 'play by play' description, but they do want me to be clear about who I am having sex with, or if I think things are moving that way. And if it does happen, I let my partners know as soon as reasonably possible. If they find out via other means, then that might feel like cheating. And even when I know It isn't, it can feel like it.

We talk about kinks and preferences. One of the advantages of poly is one partner doesn't have to enjoy everything you do. So be ok with it if they - or you - do not enjoy certain things. Share what you do enjoy.

Talk about those things that you would like to know about when your partners have sex with others. I want to know about it before it happens but that is a preference. I find it really important (almost a need) that they take a shower before they come home. And if you have a 'I want to know before you are with anyone else' and your partner has a 'none of your business' view, recognize that is a potential conflict - a big one at that.

Beyond talking, how about some simple logistics? Wash your bed sheets more often, stock up on lube and condoms. And once more, master the art of keeping the calendar up to date. If you have a sexy time date planned with one partner, respect that and don't tire yourself out with another partner. To be more blunt, I am not likely to be having intercourse twice in one night at this point in my life.

Also, keep in mind that not everyone is always in the mood. Sex should not be used as a barometer of the relationship. Sometimes we just aren't feeling it. Stress, too much drinking, lack of sleep, and a host of other things impacts drive, but you can still be intimate – intimacy does not mean sex.

(Now, just in case you read this title and thought I was going to share some 'how to pleasure your partners' tips, I'll give you one. Be mindful. Be present with who you are with. 100% there and connected and engaged. Pay attention to what you are doing right then; stop planning your next move. If you kiss lips, or an ear, or even an elbow, with complete attention and awareness, you'll build connection and intimacy and create a pretty hot time)

Dawn says...

Dan mentions that his partners don't like 'play by play' details of what he does with his partners...I do like to hear what he does and what Raymond does for that matter. BUT I realize that their partners may not want that information shared, so I don't ask. I ask for generics, like 'did you have sex?' or 'did you do bdsm play?' but that's about it. It satisfies my curiosity without them sharing too much personal information.

I do like it if I'm at least warned that sex may be happening. I don't know why it's so important, but it is, and I'm ok with feeling that way right now. I may grow out of it, it may always remain important to me. I just don't want to feel like I'm being cheated on. Secrets. Remember? Big trigger for me.

I make sure to mention this when I'm dating someone new and we are getting more serious. If we are going to be in a relationship, I need to know when they are having sex with someone else. I tell them up front, because if that's an issue for them, they need to know.

I don't care that my partners have sex with others. Well, I do, but being poly means that I mostly expect it to happen. But, to not tell me at all, especially with someone that I don't even know they are dating? Cheating. Even in poly, it happens.

There is something else I'd like to point out and that's sex during NRE (new relationship energy), with a new partner. The sex is more than likely going to be more exciting than with a partner that you have a more mature relationship with. I mean, it's new and different. But, keep that in mind and don't put your other partners on a back burner. Know that they may need more time with you as you develop more relationships and if you short change them, they may take it personally when it's not.

Some people will constantly pull in new people to keep their sex life exciting. It takes skill to keep the sex great with long term partners. Learn some skills. Learn how to keep the intimacy going with all your partners. And remember that each partner is different in what they like and don't like. Don't treat us all the same. There are things that I like that Dan's or Raymond's other partners do not. And if they confuse me with them, or worse, them with me....no one is going to be happy.

CONCERNS ABOUT STI'S

Dan says...

One of the big conversations Dawn and I had when we got started with polyamory was 'what about sexually transmitted diseases. If your monogamy was trustworthy and really did just include two people, then opening your sex life to more people increases your risk of getting a STI (sexually transmitted infection), although not fun, it is a simple truth. So far, 18 years in, Dawn and I have avoided any problems in this area, but we recognize that it is part of what we signed up for. Here are our guidelines and philosophy. As always, 'take what you want and leave the rest'.

We made that decision to have an acceptable risk. For us, this means we have looked at the possibilities and decided on agreements that reflect acceptable and unacceptable risky behavior.

Acceptable Risk (for us)

• Fingering or hand jobs, assuming your hands and clean and not injured (cuts or such) do not require protection.

• Oral, anal, and PIV (penis in vagina) do all require protection (condom, etc.).

• Fluid bonding should be taken seriously. If I decide that a girlfriend and I are now going to be fluid bonded, it impacts not only Dawn and I, but Karen and Raymond and all their fluid bonded partners as well.

• New partners are expected to understand our protection decisions and respect that. It isn't up for debate or negotiation. We are upfront with our views.

• If anyone decides to be fluid bonded with someone new, then everyone gets to re-evaluate if they want to stay in the 'fluid bonded chain', and it is a no-fault decision. If I decide to be fluid bonded with Kat, and that leads to Karen deciding to no longer be fluid bonded with me, then so be it, and no one gets "penalized". Every individual is the keeper of their own body and must do what feels right.

• We get tested. Yearly at the least, and whenever we become intimate with a new person (and they do as well).

This isn't intended to be the best or only way; it is simply what we have decided and what works for us. Having that conversation with your partner's as you explore polyamory, in an open and respectful way, will help everyone feel more secure...and have more fun.

Dawn says...

The safer sex policy that Dan describes above, doesn't work for everyone. There are many ways of doing this, but it has worked for us for over a decade. Some would say that others shouldn't have any say it what is safer sex between someone coming in and you are allowed to have your own thoughts on this, obviously. But we are very up front with how we do this and if it doesn't work for a new person coming in, they absolutely have the option not to pursue the relationship, or, let's say that my boyfriend wants to change things on his end and not use protection with someone. All I ask is that he lets me know so that I can make the decision if I'm going to stay fluid bonded with him and he gets to make the same choice with me if I decide to become fluid bonded with someone else.

So far, all of us have been open to discussing all of this and our poly pod effects many, many people.

I personally, try to get tested every 6 months or so. Yearly with my personal doctor and a second time through an event that provides testing and randomly when someone new is brought in.

As I said, this has worked for us so far and helps me feel comfortable with how large our poly pod has become over time.

POLYAMORY DOESN'T
MEAN SEX

Dan says...

Often, we might discuss polyamory, plan what it might look like, decide what a great and enlightened idea it is, and then...someone we are close to starts to have sex with someone else and things get tough. You might think it easier if polyamory wasn't about sex. Well, it isn't – directly at least, and sometimes, at all.

In some polyamorous relationships, sex isn't part of the picture at all. I personally have had three relationships, each lasting over a year, that did not include sex (that statement will include some clarification, but more about that in a moment).

So, this section is about relationships that the people involved decide that sex isn't going to be part of it. We have some friends that decided on a polyamory relationship style but some in the 'pod' identify as asexual (someone who doesn't have any sexual desires). Another two people who identify as each other's 'primary' are a male/female coupling but both identify sexually as gay; thus, although they don't have sex with each other, they are intimate with other partners. Others we know have decided due to health – one has a sexually transmitted infection. They want to stay together but chose to avoid sex for health reasons, and there are other reasons – some as simple as mismatched libidos – that sex may not be part of a poly relationship.

But in all these situations of people I've known, there is a very real level of connection and love.

As I mentioned, I've had a few relationships where sex didn't become part of things. In these cases, they all potentially had sex on the table to start, and an understanding that things might be headed in that direction, but for various reasons, they did not. Each of these relationships did include intimacy of various levels – holding hands, cuddles, or other physical expressions of connection, just not "penis in vagina" ...or penis in anything else.

These were all legitimate polyamorous relationships. The reason sex wasn't part of it varied but it wasn't the core of a relationship and thus, not that important. We sometimes hear people joke that "polyamory isn't all about the sex", in truth, it really isn't.

Dawn says...

One of the things that I like about polyamory is that I have various partners that I have sex with and love or am in love with. But, if anything happened to where they weren't interested in sex anymore, or I wasn't interested, or one of were unable for whatever reason, I'd like to think that I wouldn't give up on the relationship itself. There will be a day, as we get older, where sex will stop being interesting, or so I'm told.

Love, for me, isn't wrapped around sex. I do need intimacy from someone I'm involved in. And I absolutely need sex at this point in my life. Sex is very spiritual to me. But, that's the great thing about polyamory – if I have a partner that isn't interested in sex, I have other partners or at least the potential for other partners to have a sexual relationship with.

INTROVERTS AND METAMOURS

Dawn says...

This is another word that I wish I had found much earlier than I did: introvert.

I think it took me a long time, even though I have a psychology degree, because it got lost in other things. For one, I used to be painfully shy. This is not the same as being an introvert. Not only shy, but I'm also an abuse survivor so my shields/walls were built super tight around me. This is not the same as being an introvert.

So, what is an introvert? It's someone that recharges their energy by being alone. We find being around people or having to engage in small talk to be draining. We can do it, but it's taxing.

So, yes, I was shy. Yes, I had baggage to overcome to get my shields to relax. But my biggest revelation was finding out that I'm also an introvert. I can work on being shy and did so. I can work on my baggage and shields and did so. But, being an introvert, that's not something that can be fixed, nor should it be. By realizing this, I can explain to others and understand for myself what's going on and why I'm behaving a certain way. Then, I can work on those behaviors if they are getting in the way of the experiences I want to have. Not everything falls into this category though. Sometimes I feel the need to spend time with just me, or just one other person. Now, instead of feeling broken, I know this is because I'm an introvert and I'm ok with it.

Anyway....it would have helped me a lot more if I'd known this about myself much earlier.

For example, as Dan and I would find someone to date, he'd expect me to spend time with her on my own. (He's also an introvert by the way). I wouldn't want to spend time with someone new. It's not that anything is wrong with them. But, what do you talk about? I don't do small talk. It makes for a very awkward situation.

When Dan started dating an extrovert, Karen, she would want to go out and get pedicures or have dinner or join her book club (shiver) or.... a multitude of other things. I couldn't make myself do it. I'd much rather stay home and read or write. It really put me on the spot and caused some hurt feelings. She assumed it was because I didn't like her. I assumed there was something wrong with one of us. Because if I liked her, wouldn't I want to spend time with her? Come to find out, no. I can like people, and I do like a lot of people, it doesn't mean I want to spend time with them.

Currently, I have a couple of metamours. There are times that I forget that I should (in my poly world) be nurturing those relationships. But it's hard when you just want to be alone. Especially since most of them are extroverts, they don't necessarily understand that me wanting to be alone has nothing to do with them.

It is hard for me to build relationships with them though. I'd rather stay behind my shields and go out and do things on my own. I've tried to change how I react to situations. But, it's who I am. I've had some success with thinking myself through it.... but it's challenging.

I think my metamours have come to know me at this point and not take it personally.... I've certainly tried to be clear about it, but I'm sure it's a challenge for them as well.

Dan says...

Here are some tips for dating an introvert which I share with partners who want to date me. Although I present them as being about "me", they do seem to hold true for many of my introvert friends. Share them with your favorite extrovert!

Being around people is tiring. I am likely not going to last the whole night at a party; and if I have a place to escape to for a while that will help me stick it out.

I don't like small talk, but I do like to talk about significant things. Instead of asking me about the weather, I'd prefer you ask me about my goals or plans. And I like time to think before answering a question.

I don't like last minute changes. Give me a plan of the what and when, but activity filled schedules can become overwhelming

INTROVERTS AND EXTROVERTS

Dawn says...

Are you an introvert? An extrovert? An ambivert? Do you know? Do you care?

An introvert is someone that draws energy from being alone. They can be around people, but it can be very taxing. An extrovert, on the other hand, is someone that energizes from being around other people. Though they can spend time alone, that becomes taxing. Then there is an ambivert which can thrive with the combination of both.

This is a sliding scale though. According to Carl Jung, if someone was a complete introvert or extrovert, they'd be in a mental hospital.

So, I'm an introvert that has moments of being an extrovert. I'm an introvert that pretends very well at being an extrovert when on stage. Then, I'm charged energetically for about 15 minutes if I've gotten some interaction from the audience, before crashing and needing a nap.

This can become an issue when interacting with partners or metamours that are extroverts. I can remember Karen wanting to get together and wanting to do girly things; manicures, pedicures, massages. Eww. I don't do people. I don't do girly things with other people. If I do these things, I do them alone. I don't want to share car rides because I need a plan of escape. I don't want to engage in small talk. It bores me.

I used to think I was broken (you know, effects of past baggage and stuff), until I started running into other people like this, and not all of them had past baggage. It's just how they related to the world. Then, I realized Dan was like me. He hides it much better than I do.

One day during my reading, I came across the word 'introvert'. I had known of this word for a long time but hadn't really paid attention to it and really thought was just another word for being shy. Then, I started reading all the clues about being an introvert. OH! That's what I am. I started reading more things about introverts and realized that other things I do are because of this type of personality. Huh. It makes sense now. I wasn't rejecting people like they thought. I was just being me; an introvert.

As I read more, one thing that was mentioned was to not try to 'fix' an introvert. There isn't anything wrong with us. It's just that extroverts are usually what we see in the media, on TV, in the movies. We aren't broken. There is nothing to fix.

Extroverts don't usually know what to do with us. They invite us out and we say, 'no thanks' or maybe 'next time'. They want us to go to parties with them, which for many of us introverts is its own type of hell. But that doesn't mean an introvert/extrovert pairing won't work. Everyone just needs to be aware of what the other needs, make some compromises and remember to not take things personally, and don't try to change the other person.

If someone invites me to a party that has a lot of people attending that I don't know, be ok with me standing off a little and watching, if I show up at all. I'm not trying to be rude or stand-offish. I'm just doing what feels comfortable for me. Though, one time I did this, and someone recorded me while recording some action that was going on at the party. I came across it on Facebook and noticed myself sitting away from people during the party, just watching everyone. Well, I can see why some people would think I'm unapproachable and why the boyfriend was asking me if everything was ok. He kept texting me from across the room or the patio. I was confused because I was enjoying myself, just people watching and their shenanigans that I had no interest in taking part of. But, on the recording, I looked lonely and like I'd rather be somewhere else and that wasn't the case.

After seeing this video, I try to make myself look more approachable. I try to participate more, but it can be a challenge. I'm usually hyper focused on what I'm involved in or not wanting to be noticed unless I'm on stage.

I try to remember to tell new people that I'm an introvert. If they have any knowledge of what this means, it gives them a clue about me. If they don't know what that means, I'm happy to explain. It's easier than to be put in situations I'm not comfortable with.

Now, some introverts prefer to be with other introverts as partners, because neither is pushing the other out of their comfort zone. Each will be happy playing video games, board games, reading, and other non-people entertaining things. Though there are some that prefer to date extroverts, or otherwise they'd never get out of the house and meet new people, and some like the combination of partners.

Just remember, introverts aren't broken. There isn't anything to fix, just sometimes compromises need to be made.

Dan says...

Karen invited me to go to a holiday party at her work. I groaned - ugh, I hate those things, but I assume I would be a poor poly partner if I didn't go. and I survived. But it was so freeing to realize the simple label of being an introvert! And that Karen was an extrovert! And we related to the world differently. Another great poly moment - when invited to the holiday party, I can suggest the extroverted boyfriend will enjoy it more.

DEALING WITH HARDSHIPS

Dan says...

As of about 6 hours ago (as of when I started to write this chapter), I got laid off from my Corporate America job of the past 15 years. Yes, I mean that literally, not as a metaphor or 'this will sound good in a book'. There are a variety of emotions, mostly related to it sucking, but there is some realization that an advantage of polyamory is the support network. From the simple logical perspective, polyamory (for me) means I live with two other working adults; thus, I am not the "sole breadwinner" in the house and the impact of my loss of income will be softened by that.

Beyond the logistics, there is the even more important increased love and emotional support. I have several partners that are in touch, standing by, ready to give me space to laugh or cry or whatever I need. They are helping by reminding me I am not my job, and that I am still valued. To not over react and that, as annoying as it is to hear, there is truth in that 'when one door closes another opens'.

I honestly believe that successful long-term polyamory means that the people involved develop a level of emotional maturity. In other words, we learn to roll with the punches. I have surrounded myself with relationships that understand that love is not about what we do. They will understand that instead of eating out it will be cooking at home; Netflix instead of movie theaters; window shopping instead of...well, shopping.

I don't know what happens next career wise. I'm not overly worried about it (which might just be shock right now).

*update: after writing the above, within 28 days I found another job within the same company...with a 3% raise.

THIS TOO SHALL PASS

Dawn says...

There is this saying that I used to hear a lot that actually comes in handy when I'm having a rough time; when I'm struggling with something emotional or when I'm triggered.... "This too shall pass." It sounds cliché, but it really works.

It used to be that when my emotions felt out of control, that it would last forever. And what was the point in struggling with all of this or trying to make it work, if it was going to always feel like this? But, then, things would be better, and I'd wonder why I was making a big deal out of things.

This cycle would happen again and again: Struggle, feel the pain, work it out, feel better. And I realized that it really is a cycle. Let's say Dan is going out with someone new. I don't know what this could mean or how it's going to turn out or how it's going to affect my life, so I worry and stress over it. Maybe I use one of the other tools we've written about. But, one of them that has helped a lot is "This too Shall Pass". Just hang in there long enough for the emotions and logic to line up. It's not always going to feel like this. AND make sure not to act on the out of control emotions. Wait until the emotions settle down and cycles around. Soon, you will see that the cycles are shorter and shorter and shorter. Sometimes it's just a matter of breathing and waiting.

Sometimes, I've even found that I'm not reacting well, or in the manner that I'd like, because I'm hungry, angry, lonely or tired.... HALT. So, I make sure to eat, maybe journal, meditate or do breathing exercises, make sure to be around people if possible, or take a nap or go to bed. It helps pass time and takes care of the bio issues that may be taking place.

Dan says...

"This too shall pass" is not, as someone suggested to me, some new age adage or a Christian bible quote. I found it interesting that it originated in the writings of the medieval Persian Sufi poets.

The idea behind it - that all things are of a temporary nature - is true on many levels, but when applied to polyamory, very helpful. I have felt jealous, sad, angry, alone since starting to explore polyamory. And all those conditions are temporary. I don't feel any of them at this moment.

And it is important to apply this to the fun stuff too – new relationship energy, that moment of bliss in orgasm, seeing a lover give you 'that look' and makes your heart happy. These too are temporary. Often, I've heard people express unhappiness about a relationship that is perfectly nice and good but isn't the wild ride it once was.

Things change, things grow, and that is how it is supposed to be. So, when I am in the midst of any turmoil, sometimes that simple phrase – This Too Shall Pass – is enough to remind me not to make too big a deal out of what I am feeling at the moment.

ROLES OR PEOPLE

Dawn says...

During one of the Beyond the Love Unconferences, I decided to lead a discussion on how to find a poly partner. The idea wasn't about where to look, but how to figure out what you are looking for.

This idea came up because of how Dan and I used to do poly at the beginning of our relationship and how I see it being done currently on many poly Facebook groups. For the most part, when people put out advertisements for a poly partner, they are usually looking for someone to fill a role. Usually it's 'looking for someone to go to gaming cons with me' or 'guy and girl looking for a third to become part of the family. Must like kids and dogs and be willing to move in' or something along those lines. They are looking for someone to fill a role.

When Dan and I started out, we did some of that as well. 'Co-amorous husband and wife looking for third to join them.' We were looking for a third, which means we were looking for someone to fulfill a role. We had dreamt up this fantasy role and were looking for someone that would fit. We still do this sometimes - look for someone to fill a role - on an individual basis. At least I do.

So, when you are looking for other people, do you have that fantasy role that you would love to find a person for? 'Responsible, kid-friendly, dominant male that loves wine tours and traveling,' for example or 'Kink-friendly, artist with a sense of humor'. Anything like this usually means that we are trying to fill a role in our lives. Nothing wrong with that if we are being honest with everyone.

But, over time, through the Universe having a sense of humor at my expense, I found another way of finding a partner.

I had just broken up with someone that I'd dated for a while that had found me through the podcast. They were cute, had a great smile, so what the hell. But it didn't go so well. They just weren't a match There were too many differences and I just wasn't happy.

So, after the break-up, I created a list of what I wanted in the new person that I thought I'd be happy with - 'dominant, knows who he is, can hold a conversation, spiritual, sense of humor' and I think I had a couple other things on there as well.

Then, I started looking. Well, a specific list like this can be hard to fill but I trusted that the Universe had my best interest at heart.

At one point, I ran across someone at our local poly group and heard him talk about how he was finding it hard to find someone. I asked around about him, found someone he used to date and called her to get his information. Then, I called him and asked him out for coffee. He asked that we not read each other's profiles on social media before having coffee. I was good with that.

It was hard not to sneak a peek at his profile, but I take pride in being honest and trustworthy so honored the request. We had coffee.

I'm not a normal person that dates. I hate small talk and I hate wasting time. I really don't like playing the dating game, because I never really learned how to play it. So, on this date I turned the conversation to some heavy topics after it looked like we would get along. We sat in the coffee shop for a couple of hours and talked about the big-gun topics you are told to never talk about on a first date. Well, I have some things about me that are part of my life that might turn some people off, so I like to get them on the table right away, and as it turns out, so did he.

I'm so glad we didn't read each other's profiles, because if we had, we would never have met for coffee.

The Universe laughs. I got what I asked for. But everything I asked for, he's on the opposite end of the spectrum from me. My spiritual path has me on one end, and his has him on the other end. This is usually non-compatible. My political views have me on one end and his has him on the other. This is usually non-compatible. Oh, he can hold his own in a conversation and is well-educated.... more so than me. That's going to be (and has been) a challenge.

But what we found out during that talk was that we could have a conversation. Even though we think differently and even as opposites, we can still relate intimately and have a loving relationship. I'm glad we didn't see who each other was on paper. And I'm glad we pulled out the big guns to talk about on a first meeting. It showed me who he was as a person, and that's what I needed to see. If I'd read his profile first, I may have decided that he wouldn't fit in the role that I had created in my head. Raymond and I have now been together more than 5 years.

So, when the next person came along, I decided to just let the relationship be what it was, not to shove them into a role that I'd been dreaming of. During our time together, someone would ask me who they were and how they fit in my life, and I wouldn't have an answer. They just became part of my life; they still don't have a label.

So, you need to look at what you are looking for, or if you are even actively looking for that matter.

Are you looking for someone to fill a role? Many people think that a current partner isn't supposed to fill all the roles, and with polyamory, instead of dumping the current partner, we are allowed to look for another. So, are you looking for someone to fill a role? or are you more organic with your polyamory? This means that you are open to feeling feelings about someone and then just allowing them to fit into your life how they may. For example: meeting someone at a social gathering, getting to know them, but the details don't really matter. If the feelings are there, you'll figure out how to make it work.

Though, I do have a few requirements that are non-negotiable, regardless of whether the person fits a role or is more organic. They must be honest, trustworthy and be ok with my power exchange relationship with my husband. I discuss all this right out of the gate as well, including what I mean by honest and trustworthy since we all have our own ways of defining those words.

Want to know a little secret? For me, I must admit that I still have a concept of the 'perfect' person to fit a role I have in mind. Does this come from starting out in the swinger and kink communities where you are allowed and expected to describe your 'wants and needs' for who you are looking for? "Are you looking for a top? A bottom? A great flogger? An energy player? Maybe soft swap? Full swap?" These are questions that are negotiated before those types of relationships because they are looking for someone compatible in a role. So, I've done a lot of thinking about what I'd like in a partner. I have a long list of needs and wants for myself and what I'm looking for in life.

As for the role I'd like to fill, I dream about it and tweak it every now and then as I learn something new about myself or discover a new interest. I don't ask the Universe for it again though, because even though they did well by me that last time, regardless of their sense of humor, I'm not so sure I want to put that out there again. So, instead, I stay open to more organic meetings and if feelings develop, I'll see how the new person fits into my life. And I keep an eye out for a person that might want to fill the role (or two) that I have in mind.

Dan says...

I'm not looking for any new partners today; I've got a full plate, lots of love, and am happy with the balance in my life. But I am also aware that a person might pop into my view that doesn't fulfill any role or desire, and at this point in my life, that sounds like a lot of fun. I call this "the stranger", the person you don't expect to show up and suddenly you are dating someone new and have no idea where it is going and to me, today, that just feels like a great adventure.

ABUNDANCE VS SCARCITY

Dawn says...

There is this thought that if we operate from the place of abundance instead of scarcity, it will be much easier to be gracious and generous with our time, our resources, our partners.

It's the idea that love is not in limited supply. That the more love there is, the more we can generate. Therefore, if one of my partners falls in love with someone else, it doesn't mean that it dries up the supply that is pointed my way.

But, at least for me, I was raised with the idea that there are so many good men out there and you need to grab one and do whatever it takes to keep them. And if they turn their eye to someone else, you've lost your supply of love. Scarcity. Not enough resources, not enough love, fight for every scrap you can get.

That's not true when it comes to polyamory relationships though. There is plenty to share. So, I've decided to change my thinking from that which was drilled into me. I want to come from a place of abundant love.

Dan says...

What a gift we can offer to ourselves and to each other when we operate from abundant love. It means that we rejoice when a partner finds a new lover instead of clinging because we fear loss. It might take a lot of work to reprogram yourself - as Dawn said, most of us are not raised to think this way. For me, I had to experience it to really believe it. But seeing Dawn find a new boyfriend and having that energy flow over to our relationship was all the evidence I needed.

HOW TO MEET PEOPLE

Dan says...

Some would say that being polyamorous isn't about the number of partners you have; that you can be in a two-person relationship or even single and not dating anyone and still identify as polyamorous. And although I agree with this, polyamory in action is about having partners. So where do we meet all these poly people to get those multi partner relationships going?

Before we get into that part, I am going to share a bit of a point of contention for me. I often hear people say, "I can't find anyone to date because I'm _____". And at some point, everything fills in the blank. My experience as an average looking married male has been that I don't have enough time for all the people who would like to be in my life. Other people in my shoes say no one is interested in dating married males. They say 'it would be easy if they were a sexually active female' – and yet Dawn has gone for long periods of not being able to find anyone (and she would very much enjoy being...well, more sexually active and relationship active as well).

I've heard people say that they can't find partners because they are single, married, trans, straight, asexual, demi sexual, male, female, various racial and ethnic backgrounds, and more. And I personally know people who are all the above and actively poly and in relationships.

Now, I'm not saying that all things are equal. And I will say it is true that if you are a male who is only attracted to other males then your pool of potential partners is smaller. But the first step in finding new partners is to stop saying "I can't find anyone because I'm _____". The next steps we've outlined below.

In Real Life

The most likely place you'll meet people who identify as polyamorous is of course polyamory focused events. From the local munch to the bigger polyamory events, I've had the most luck meeting partners at poly themed gatherings. Sometimes they create social situations just for this purpose. At the yearly Beyond the Love event, we include both a flirt board and mixers just to make meeting people easier. And even when the reason for the gather isn't anything to do with starting new relationships, you are after all surrounding yourself with poly minded people.

The next best place (in my experience) has been attending events that may not be poly but are friendly to an alternative view. We really do understand that not all people are polyamorous and (kinky/gamers/etc.). But I've met partners at kink events and many friends tell me relationships started at gaming conventions and other gathers that run from Leather (gay BDSM) to LARPing (live action role play games). In the above events people in general have more of an open mind and open attitude, though not poly events, they are often poly friendly.

From here, it can get tricky. Using resources like Meet-Up or other social gathering or even at work to meet people have all worked for me, but then how you approach the polyamory part is challenging. On one hand, I only date people who are poly friendly. On the other hand, leading with "Your cute, want to meet my wife?" can be confusing for people - and although polyamory is more in the news and media that it used to be, we certainly can't call it "mainstream" and people's impression of it can be based on some unrealistic models.

When you speak up and tell someone you are poly is a matter of various opinions. I tend to lean toward 'early and gentle'. 'Early' as in at the point I realize I'm about to ask the person out on a date - or as soon as they seem to be ready to ask me. By 'gentle', I mean by asking them a question or two that will help me ascertain if they are familiar with the idea of polyamory at all (and might give me a sense for how they view it).

My favorite gentle question is "Have you seen the show Married and Dating?" You can ask about Sister Wives or Big Love as well, although those are more about polygamy, which might muddle the waters some. If they answer yes, you can say something like "I don't think most polyamorous people look like them; what do you think?". If they answer No, then you can respond with something around the idea of "The gist of the show is that some relationships include more than two people, in a loving and consensual way. What do you think about that?" In either case, I've had people respond with everything from 'That is a sin against (my belief system)' to the far more fun 'speaking of which, let me tell you about my husband...'.

Once you have met someone, then how you proceed is a different question. Refer to our chapter on Poly Flirting.

Online
Although you can try alt sites like Fetlife or Swingtowns or even those couple of dating sites that suggest they are poly friendly. Most of the success stories we hear involve OKCupid. They have a lot of matchmaking questions that focus on monogamy, so if you answer those in a poly-friendly way (and mark it as mandatory) it will help sort through people. There is also a Chrome plugin called

'OKCupid for the non-mainstream user', It will let you filter by non-monogamous preferences.

Dawn says...

Dan covered most of the points of how to meet people, I'd like to throw a few more out there. I've had luck in meeting people as alternative spiritual events as well; drumming circles, hook suspensions, and other pagan festivals. If there are any gatherings of CAW (Church of All Worlds) around, part of their foundation is on poly relationships. All of these are great places to meet people, though remember that not everyone there will be polyamorous, but most will at least be poly aware.

And if you meet someone online, remember to follow through with the dates. Don't ghost people (we used to call that 'standing someone up' as in 'I got stood up'). You can't really start a relationship with someone if you aren't willing to take the chance and actually meet them. I know it can be scary. Hell, I've been doing this for years and I still got nervous last week when I went on a coffee date with someone from one of those online sites.

Oh, and being from the kink community, we used to have this thing called 'safe calls'. I don't hear too many people doing those anymore. But they were calls that we made while on a date to let someone know that we were ok. If we didn't make the call on time, our safe call person was to call the police. Remember to be safe. Make smart choices. Let people know who you are meeting and where. Meet in public. Don't get into someone's car. Hell, I don't even allow them to walk me to my car. Maybe it's a girl thing, but I park under a bright light if it's dark out and if I'm going to give a hug, I do so outside of the establishment and walk myself to my car. If they offer, I just say that it's ok, I've got it. They may just be trying to be chivalrous, but I don't know this person. I try to meet someone for coffee first, during the day in a place that I'm comfortable with. I can usually pick up a vibe at that point.

So, one previous partner I met through our podcast. I met Raymond through Poly Columbus, our local poly support group. I met my girlfriend at a kink event. I have a couple of play partners that I only see at kink events. I met someone I'm interested in at a Tantra meetup, and another that I just met from an online site. It's getting easier and easier to meet like-minded people. I just make sure to attend events that are poly-friendly.

SOMETIMES YOU HAVE TO LEAVE SOMEONE OUT

Dan says...

Karen took me to her work Christmas party one year and her co-worker said, "Nice to finally meet you Larry" and another co-worker said "Shh, that is Chris!" before Karen spoke up, saying "No, this is the other one, Dan". Karen is openly poly at work, and I found the entire thing amusing. Later that year, there was a company-sponsored carnival, where she brought both Larry and I and one of Larry's children.

But sometimes you just can't include all your partners in different events, gathering, or holidays. It might be due to simple logistics, such as only have two tickets to something or long-distance relationships, or it can be a situation where the decisions are made that you are not "out" with family or at work and that taking both boyfriends to a party would raise too many questions. You might have the challenging situation that your metamours just don't get along. Other times, it is just a decision that feels like it is the loving or respectful thing for it to be an event for one on one time - for example, on two people's anniversary, they might want time with just each other. That doesn't mean you (or they) are not poly - it means they are expressing love in a way that celebrates one aspect of a relationship.

Regardless of the why, sometimes you just can't be with all the ones you love. And that can be very painful - for you, but also (and often, more so) for the person not there.

What I find valuable to is to make sure that, if I am the partner that can't be with my lovers, is to stop thinking about what I can't have (be with my partners) and instead think of it as an opportunity for what I can have. From a solo bike ride, to playing board games with friends I haven't seen lately, to going to those movies that no one else likes, to random coffee with people I've wanted to get to know better. All of these are things I enjoy doing, so off I go. I can miss my partner without being stuck in that (or in other words, missing my partner isn't who I am, it is just one of the many things I feel).

If I am the partner who can't include someone, then I try to remember to reserve them some energy and let them know they are respected and missed. This can be a little bit of time to reach out to and say hi, or even a quick picture. I avoid hiding anything – that is, if we are having a good experience, then be honest about that. This does sometimes result in the away partner feeling envy, but that is an ok human emotion. By expressing it, you can avoid it feeling like jealousy.

Dawn says...

It would be wonderful if we could take all our partners with us all the time, but it's just not feasible. We live with Karen, so it's easier to take her, but Raymond lives 90 miles away with his wife and kids. My girlfriend now lives a couple of states away. And if we brought the poly pod to every event, that's a lot of people at this point. So, where do we draw the line?

Well, it depends on the event. Sometimes, I only want to do things with Dan. Or only with Raymond or only with the girlfriend. It doesn't make sense to have everyone tag along. I have a concert coming up that I'd like to go to. I'm thinking I'm only inviting one person to go with me. It's going to depend on whose available. Then there are times where we pick a movie and invite everyone to it. Sometimes we have a dinner at home and only want to invite a few.

It really depends on the situation and my mood. There are times that Raymond has gatherings at his house. I don't expect to be invited to them all. It's nice when I am, but it's not an expectation. Sometimes they go out with her other partners. Sometimes I'm invited, sometimes not. Sometimes Dan is invited with me if I'm invited, and sometimes Karen is invited with Dan when Dan is invited with me, and sometimes not. We go with the flow and remember not to take things personally. Sometimes it's as simple as there isn't enough room at the dinner table.

WHEN TO LEAVE

Dan says...

A few years into polyamory, I had a great relationship going with someone named Carol. We had some months together and things were great, and then a thing between us happened and I had to tell her I could not see her anymore.

The idea for this section was to share some insight around how to tell when it was clear that either a budding relationship wasn't going to happen or when it would be smart to terminate an existing relationship. After all, although most of what we are sharing about in this book are the ways we have made polyamory and relationships work, not all relationships are destined to make it. So, when is it time to throw in the towel and move on?

After trying to write this a few times, I've had to step back and realize that I can't give you simple 'if this happens, then you should leave' answer. Because I can't recommend you view things that way. My first start was 'if they cheat, then leave' (and by cheating, I mean that your partner has sex, intentionally hid that from you, and had no intention of revealing). But is that 100% always the right way to respond to cheating? If one of my partners of 10 years who never did anything like that before got drunk one night and made a stupid mistake, would I just say, 'we are done'? Perhaps.

About as close to an absolute I can get is "if your partner is abusing you, then yes, you should leave". Beyond that, are there any non-negotiables?

For clarity sake, we are not talking casual hookups or light dating in this section. For those, if it isn't fun, then sure, move on. But for long term loving relationships, the reality is that it isn't going to be fun all the time. Not only have we faced tears and arguments as part of our own struggles, but life happens – and that includes pets dying, jobs being lost, people getting ill, and even more serious life events. Our relationships include those as well. So, we don't advise breaking up because things are hard or 'got real' or isn't all fun and sex. Life is hard. Sometimes, with the right partner – or partners – those events are a little easier.

So, when should we give the relationship the good old 'heave ho'? Well, don't misunderstand what I've said so far, because there are times to end relationships. But instead of saying 'if this happens, you should leave', I want to present it instead as aspects of a relationship that, if they are not there, then moving on should be an option you seriously entertain.

One aspect could be a partner isn't putting energy into growth. I once heard that 'polyamory is about facing all your unresolved issues' and it does have a ring of truth about it. I had to face my fears about being alone, my jealousy, my perceived sexual inadequacy, and everything else within me that I've avoided in my monogamous relationships. Not to say that some monogamous relationships are not growth based...but mine were not. So, if I want to spend time with a lover and another partner says "Ok, but they have to stay out of the state we live in", then I need to be able to express that this isn't viable, and I'll assist my partner with why they have this feeling. I might even say "Ok, this time, we can do that", but only if we agree that this is something that we address. The issue isn't geographical, it is something else - fear, possessiveness, envy even - and I want to know my partner is willing to examine themselves.

Another one to pay attention to is intent. For me, this one is huge. If my partner says, "you can't have sex with them", the intent behind that statement is what I look at. If the intent is to piss on my parade or just be controlling or they are having a shitty day, then I am more likely to wonder if I can maintain a long-term relationship with them. If the intent is that they are also interested in that same person and don't want me cock blocking them; or that they are afraid that I won't want to be with anyone else after that; or that they heard the person has an STI and wants to discuss precautions first, then that is an intent that I might not like (or I might appreciate), but it doesn't impact our long-term relationship options.

Also, a danger sign for me is when my ethics are being either questioned or challenged. I have a sense of right and wrong. It isn't based on religion or society moral norms; but it is mine and I know it in my heart. When you ask me to do things that oppose that, then I need to look strongly at how long we might be together. I need to be heard and listened to and to be able to hear you. If you can't find a way to communicate, then the clock is ticking on your relationship I'm sorry to say.

Finally, energy. I don't expect my relationships to be easy or without challenges or free of disagreements (or even big old arguments on occasion). But I do want to feel like we are both putting in the same amount of energy to move forward. I don't need you to be poly awesome all the time - I just need to know that you are trying and that you are as interested in the growth of self and the relationship as I am.

Dawn says...

I'm not always sure what would make me break up with someone. With the ex, it's literally because we grew in opposite directions and neither were happy. I had found open relationships; kink, my spiritual path and none of those were compatible with him anymore. So, we parted.

Later I had a boyfriend that cheated. He literally met someone else, hid the relationship from me, and took her to a hotel. Told me a week later and then said the reason why he didn't tell me beforehand was because of the reaction I was having. No, I was having a bad reaction because I was just finding out that he'd developed a relationship with someone else, had slept with her and not even given me a clue that this was going on. This was after blowing me off at the last minute when we would have evening dates planned or even weekends planned. This wasn't the type of relationship I wanted in my life, so, we parted.

I do know that I need honesty in my relationships. I need transparency to a degree. I don't need to know everything, but I do need to know things that will affect our relationship. Or, as I've said before, it feels like there are secrets and that's not a feeling that I want in my life. So, if that happened with any of my partners, and it wasn't fixable, that would be a deal breaker for me.

There are other things that would be deal breakers, that would end a relationship, but I would hope I'd find that out about the person before falling in love. We can't always control the timing of our emotions though, can we? For instance, if I feared someone, it would be time to leave, or if someone tried to come between me and any of my other relationships, more than likely that could be a deal breaker. Though, intent has a lot to do with that.

Just like I can't be with someone where everything has to do with them. I can't be with a selfish person. It's needs to be a partnership of some sort.

BREAKING UP WHEN POLY

Dan says...

Being broken up with sucks for monogamous people. I'm sorry to say it sucks for polyamory people as well. Now, there can be some benefits to poly in this regard – a partner might break up with me, but I may have other partners to help me through the transition. Although it still sucks, at least the lonely part can be abated, but that isn't always the case, and even when it is, some aspects of poly breakups are different - and some would contend, worse - than typical monogamous breakups. This section deals with the turmoil of being with someone and then having a break up that results in that person (or if breaking up with a couple, triad, etc., people) no longer part of our life.

When relationships end, either at our choice or at our partners, we not only lose that person/people in our life, but we lose a number of other relationships as well.

- We lose the presence of the specific person/people.
- We lose the "Us". This is what I call that energy or entity that occurs when you and they are together. I've noticed that when I am with Karen, I have a different view and perspective than, for example, when I am with Dawn. And vice versa. One isn't better than the other, but when I am visiting a furniture store with Karen we might come across a couch and think 'that would be perfect for Saturday afternoon cuddling'. With Dawn, seeing the same couch might lead me to think 'that would be perfect to tie you down to for kinky stuff'. Both reflect aspects of my authentic self, but just like my focus and presence at work is different than it is at home, the same is true when I am interacting with my friends that have a lot of spirituality interest vs my friends that have a lot of sports interest. And with my loving partners.
- We often lose metamours. I try to develop relationships with the other people in my partner's life, and often these become friendships on their own legs.

But if Karen were to break up with me, it would be uncomfortable to go to her boyfriend's house and hang out.

That is a lot of loss and it doesn't include all the logistics, friends, and many other details that can come up when you lose a significant relationship.

So, what can you do about it?

One important step is to grieve. If you instigated the break up or it "happened to you", grieving is still a great first step. Now that might mean a few hours of being bummed out to a few days of going through boxes of Kleenex. Either way, let it happen. Recognize it ("I am sad because they moved on") but give yourself permission to be sad. The only trick is to make sure you recognize it; and that means at some point, are you still sad because they are gone (which is a fact, how things are) or are you sad because you wish things were different than they are? Be careful not to get stuck in the trap of living in the past (things used to be so great) or in the future (maybe one day they will come back). Both of those states will keep you trapped in feeling bad now.

A Buddhist would suggest that being sad is fine, but at some point, you realize suffering is optional, and that we must live in the present.

Another important step is to realize that being alone doesn't mean lonely. Be alone and be ok with being alone. Ok, I know, it isn't easy sometimes, but if your self-identity is "Joe's boyfriend" or "Kim and Phil's partner" then you will always be in danger of losing yourself. Take the steps needed to become "Dan. Who happens to be in a relationship with..." This is a tricky bit of business but essential. The steps on how to do this are addressed in depth throughout this book but you can start with something as simple making a list of things you like to do...and then make plans to do them. Is it 'Go to a movie with Paul' that you miss, or is it 'Go to a movie with a boyfriend'? Or maybe it is simply 'go to a movie with a friend' or 'Go to a movie'? Sometimes we feel weird doing things alone.

Recognize that and check in - is the only thing weird about having lunch alone that you worry what other people are thinking? Again, this is just a start, but make your mantra that being alone isn't bad. And to be honest, there are some great benefits to it. What will I have for dinner tonight? Whatever I want.

Finally, regarding this part, allow me to offer this saying – "A year from now, everything will be different". Change is, as you've heard a million times, constant. When we feel crappy right now, we tend to forget that, but it is still true. So, keep it in your mind that no matter what you are going through today, it will change. We don't know if it will be better, worse, or very similar...but different is guaranteed. So, don't attach to today too much.

Dawn says...

The breakup of my previous monogamous marriage was very different than the one I had with a poly partner. Both of these relationships weren't really healthy for me in the end, but the monogamous marriage one, I stayed with as long as I possibly could out of a sense of duty and obligation - for the kids, for the dream of the white picket fence, because it would hurt my husband's feelings if I left, because my mom stayed with my dad even though she wasn't happy, because that's what you do, because divorce would shame the family, because divorce would shame my mom. There were so many perceived obligations. But there came a day that I just couldn't do it anymore. I put 14 years into that relationship because to do anything else would be considered a failure.

Once I was living a polyamorous life, and it was time to break up with a previous boyfriend - which was his idea, but I was totally on board - it was much different. I didn't feel like I had to put up with someone else's breaking of the agreements we had made. I didn't feel like I was going to be alone for the rest of my life. I certainly didn't feel like I had to stay in the relationship. I had options that I didn't feel I had in the previous marriage. It was much easier to make healthier choices for myself with my relationships.

So, I'm not sure that the break-ups are 'easier'. I mean, there is still love and dashed dreams involved. But, for me there is a sense of freedom to know that I have more options than serial monogamy. More options than finding the next 'one' to spend the rest of my life with. Instead, I can have relationships with people that may 'transition' into something different.

I've had one relationship that did not 'transition', it ended because of a break in trust. But others have transitioned into friendships or mentoring relationships. I'm still friends with some (not all) of my ex-metamours. It's hard to give up some of those relationships just because we don't share a partner anymore.

So far, my breakup with the polyamorous partner was very different than with the monogamous one. Was it because one was for 14 years and one was only a year? Was it because one involved kids and one didn't? Was it because one broke trust and one was just because we had moved on? (It's easier for me to break up with someone that I've lost trust in. Slash. Gone. The one with my ex-husband, where we had just moved on, was more difficult because I didn't have a truly specific reason to make the decision to leave).

Was the polyamorous one easier because I had someone to turn to? Maybe it just was what it was. A future break-up could be much different.

GENEROSITY AND GRACIOUSNESS

Dan says...

As a partner of mine moves from "I'm going on a date with some new guy" to some indicator that it is an honest to goodness relationship blooming, I can go through a variety of emotional states. These can come out as fear or anger or self-doubt or many others. The tool I use to create an emotional counterbalance is to be generous and gracious. Note that I said not to feel but to be. But let me back up a moment and explain why there is an issue in the first place.

I like polyamory and believe it is the right lifestyle for me and for my partners. So, it isn't the polyamory that is an issue, but instead, it is about change, about things will not only be different, but I am not sure in what direction it will go, and I dig in and am resistant. Even though I don't really know what kind of change is coming – it could be anything from occasional dates to vacations to I'd like him to move in. I try to imagine what that change might be but in truth, we really don't know. I've dated people that I thought would be The Next Big Things fizzile out in a week; I have a relationship now that I thought was going to be an occasional date and would burn out fast that is about to celebrate a four-year anniversary.

And not only do you not know how it is going to go, you can't stop it. Granted, you can say "No, I forbid it". But forbidding them will at best lead to resentment and is a temporary solution. You can say you will leave if they continue to pursue a relationship – but if that is our first response, should we be hitched up to a poly train to start with?

So, the tool I practice is to be generous and gracious. I am honest with my partner as well - 'honey, this is really scary for me, so I hope you'll make some time to help me as I work through jealousy' and such. But I also practice putting myself in their shoes as well. If I found something – relationship or not - that I thought might be fulfilling or even just neat to try, I would want my partners to support me, not just grudgingly accept it.

For me, this means that when a partner comes home from a date, I take some deep breaths and greet them with a smile if I can, or at least a hug and hello. I ask them how the time with the other person went and just listen. In my head I might hear the voices of panic – "how will this impact me!?" – but I let that wait and just hear them. Be present and listen and smile as I can. When they say, 'We had a nice dinner' or 'saw a great movie' or 'walked on the beach', express how nice that must have been, just like if it was your friend instead of your lover (because for me, my lovers are also my friends).

Now sometimes I must 'fake it till you make it'. I put on my best calm face and mentally grind my teeth and leave my fears in check. But it really seems to be valuable to think about being gracious and generous; that drives me toward being gracious and generous. At some point, when appropriate, I will express that I am having a difficult time and want help. But I also focus on doing my best to be supportive and loving and expect the same from them.

I LOVE MY PARTNER
BUT NOT MY
METAMOUR

Dan says...

I have some metamours – partners of my partners – that I enjoy spending time with; we have common interest (beyond who we date) and we can hold a relaxed conversation about a range of topics. Some of my metamours (sometimes just called "metas") I have less in common with, but we can still be around each other and talk about work or other 'lite' topics without any issue.

And other metas...well, sometimes a partner will date someone that makes me think 'really? You see something in that person?'. This section is about how to navigate those situations.

You might be in a situation where you have a metamour you don't at all get along with but still think it is easy – perhaps they are long distance, or you don't share common time together (like let's have everyone get together for a holiday party). You might take the approach of simply ignoring it. That actually isn't normally a good strategy as the line between ignoring someone and (creating a wall around communication) is thin. After all, I don't want to have a negative response just because a name is mentioned in conversation.

Sometimes we are in a situation though where ignoring isn't an option. If your partner lives with a meta or you are all part of the same gaming group, avoidance isn't going to work out. We hope this section helps with all these situations.

Let's start off with this understanding – everyone is different. We all have personality types we mesh with and those we don't. I can name a few people at my job that I would be happy to never have to interact with. But the job, like my metamours, is an example of a situation where I do have to interact with someone regardless of my preference. So, start off there - everyone is different. Accept that.

Accept that nobody gets on with everyone, and that's okay. It doesn't mean you're a bad person, and it doesn't mean they are either.

Next, be aware of your own emotions. If someone is rubbing you the wrong way, recognize those feelings. Don't think about the person but instead the emotion. Work on that instead of engaging with the person.

Along with the above, if you can treat people respectfully, you can be part of the solution instead of part of the problem.

Finally, you'll find information elsewhere in this book about meditation. Take a glance at it; this can be a great ally in the way we react to people – and keeping it from escalating.

POLYAMORY AND GEEKY

Dan says...

Often people ask about where to meet polyamory people. The answers vary, but the funny thing is often when the question is 'where did you meet your new partner?', the answer is something related to geek culture! From board game meetups, to comic conventions, to Star Trek movie marathon nights at the local alt theater, there is a lot of mix between the geek and polyamory communities.

Now, this isn't to say this isn't true in other cultures as well (it is) nor are we suggesting that everyone you meet at a polyamory meetup can name the last two Dr. Who's or has ever heard about Settlers of Catan (a popular board game). But when we ran the polyamory convention we created (Beyond the Love) for six years, the Saturday night Board Game room was very well attended!

We like to say, "Polyamory is how we live; geeky is how we play". And to explore some polyamory themed games, check out Choice of the Pirate, Fable, or Amber's Magic Shop just to name a few! And head over to boardgamegeek.com and check out the Microbadge for Polyamorous!

Dawn says...

It is kind of funny how many of my poly partners or poly people that I know are also geeky. Maybe some of us found polyamory because of our geekiness? If you ask Poly/Geeky people if they've read 'Stranger in a Strange Land'[2] by Robert Heinlein, there is usually a resounding 'yes!'. The main character in this book had loving relationships with multiple women and for some of us, that was the first time we came across the idea that this could be used as a normal model for relationships. Of course, he was raised on a different planet, so was raised with different ideas...but what if we could do that here on Earth as well? Obviously, many of us ran with the idea.

Are some of us poly and geeky because we have creative minds? Or that it's easy for us to live in fantasy worlds? There are a lot of us that are 'table toppers'. In other

[2] Robert A. Heinlein, Stranger in a Strange Land

words, we play table top games like Dungeons and Dragons, Savage Worlds, GURPs, and so on. Or we are LARPers, Live Action Role Players. We create fantasy worlds, create costumes for our characters in the game and then meet on weekends at camps we've rented and spend the whole weekend as our characters. I've had fun in both worlds, and my kids hate when I admit to it. Their mom is already weird enough, but to be a middle aged LARPer and table topper? It's easier for them to deal with the other things I am.

The trick is, to take all this interest in fantasy worlds and realize that when we are creating the fantasy world of 'polyamory', that it takes more than the roll of the dice, the draw of a card or the throwing of a spell to work with the emotions that are part of real relationships. That's where our tools come into play.

POLYAMORY AND POWER EXCHANGE

Dan says...

Polyamory is a relationship style that includes multiple loving relationships. It can take many forms, but overall, that is polyamory in a nutshell.

Power Exchange (PE) is a relationship style that is designed to have a hierarchal leader/follower structure. There is a person who is in charge; anyone else recognizes that the other person is in charge. Like polyamory, there are many styles of power exchange and they go by many different names – Dom/sub*, Master (or Mistress or Ma'am)/slave, Queen/knight, Owner/property, Leader/follower, and others. If you are unfamiliar with power exchange, the first thing to share is these are consensual relationships. You may want to do some exploration before jumping to the conclusion that they are unhealthy or abusive. I can personally introduce you to dozens of long-term (and joyful) PE relationships. For actual reflections of how it is done day to day by real people, we recommend our book Living M/s[3].

You might be wondering if you can practice both polyamory and power exchange. Well, the answer is yes. As a matter of fact, if you go to a kink-based event, you'll see many people practicing it.

Here are some specific thoughts, tips, and call outs about this sort of relationship combination.

First off, as you explore the polyamory part, expect some pushback from non-power exchange polyamory followers. Some aspects of power exchange, such as rule-based relationship, one person getting final say (including veto power), and at times, one person can have additional partners but the other can't, might be part of a negotiated power exchange. And those items are often considered poor relationship ideas by those that practice non-hierarchal polyamory. That viewpoint is what it is. These aspects might be fine and functional in Power Exchange + Polyamory

[3] Dan and Dawn Williams, Living M/s; A Book for Masters, slaves, and Their Relationships

relationships. Sometimes it is exactly what all parties want. Power Exchange relationships (when they are done ethically) are done with a lot of negotiations before any power is exchanged.

Next, if you are looking for PE & Poly friendly events, pay attention to the kink & Leather communities. Although you might not be kinky, you'll find they often include polyamory tracks. There is a lot of crossover.

Finally, I'll tell you about a huge and painful mistake I hope you can avoid. If you are an existing power exchange couple, you might be tempted to cut back a bit on PE as you explore a new outside love relationship. Perhaps you'll treat your submissive as more of a peer because you want to be certain that being poly was truly OK with them and they didn't just accept it because you are the Top. Don't. Instead, make it part of the power exchange. Perhaps have them pack a bag when you go off to the home of another significant other, so they are in direct service to you as part of your other relationship.

*I'll note that in the case of this section of the book, we are using the term Dom/sub as a power exchange relationship type. It is also sometimes used to reflect who is in charge in the bedroom.

Dawn says...

Coming across someone that is Polyamorous and in a Power Exchange relationship can be confusing for some people. It was confusing for us at first, as well. I had agreed to and even helped create the contract that we put together for our power exchange relationship. Now, we were adding in new people, some of who were also part of our hierarchical structure and some who were not.

Honestly, when we talk about 'porch time' in our classes, it's usually during our Power Exchange classes. This is the communication tool we created so that we wouldn't harm our power exchange structure as we added in other relationships. According to what I wanted/needed and documented in our contract, I didn't want to disrespect my other partners by yelling when I was out of control with emotions. That's what I did in my last long-term relationship, but I also needed to be 'heard' in my Power Exchange relationship. As an external processor, I really need to be heard and to not feel like I was allowing myself to be a doormat just because I'm his submissive.

So, we built Porch Time so that we could leave our hierarchical structure for some time and have these hard discussions. Then, when we came to an agreement of how to handle something as peers, we'd go back to our hierarchical relationship. I'm a happy girl once again.

For me, any new relationship that I have, they must be aware that I'm in a Power Exchange relationship with Dan. Some people that don't understand power exchange may think this is unfair, but my current partners are totally ok with this. For me, it was about finding the right other partners.

Raymond and the girlfriend are ok with it, because they are familiar with the kink community and have experienced pieces of power exchange themselves. When I told Raymond, that Dan has Veto power, he had to take some time and think if he wanted to be in a relationship with me, knowing the ax could drop. So, he got to know Dan and realized that Dan wouldn't veto for any old reason. Even when things started going downhill with the last boyfriend, Dan didn't veto. He watched, to make sure I was safe, and then let me come to the realization that the relationship was no longer healthy and then go through the breakup. So, yes, Dan has consensual veto power with me, but he's not a dick with that power.

Personally, I like that he has veto power. I like that feeling of being watched over and being taken care of, but also knowing that he trusts my judgment enough not to use it unless absolutely necessary. And if you are wondering, no, I don't have the same veto power. I like the feeling of being a submissive to someone that I absolutely trust. Honestly, it's my kink and helps me sit in my seat of power (I explain this better in our book, Living M/s). Having veto power takes that feeling away from me. That feeling is hard to explain if you don't get it. It's ok. I'm perfectly happy with this arrangement and it's worked for me for 20 years. It feeds me, and I know this combination of Polyamory and Power Exchange feeds others as well.

POLYAMORY AND LEATHER

Dawn says...

One of the first places we ran across people living in polyamorous relationships was in the Leather Community. If you aren't sure what the Leather community is, it has a fascinating history. It used to be comprised of gay males that would meet in certain bars, seeking male companionship after WW II (and some hot leather sex). Over time, women were allowed in, beginning in the 1980's during the AIDs crisis. By the time Dan and I stumbled into the community, it was much more hetero-friendly.

Dan and I were interested in learning about kink, and NLA (National Leather Association) was the only thing that we could find available in our area. We had just moved in together and the internet was just becoming more readily available so that we could find groups.

So, we started going to NLA group functions and parties and started paying attention to the relationships that were around us. It was fascinating to see all the combinations that we hadn't been exposed to before. I mean, we had read about them and fantasized about so many things, but now we were involved with a community that had people in it that were living our fantasy life.

And they used their own labels or didn't have labels at all. Many of us didn't know the word 'polyamorous' at this time. The word had only been around for a few years when we were starting out. 'Open relationship' and 'swinging' and 'play partners' was used much more often in our area.

I can remember playing with a couple at a house party of theirs and Dan making the comment that it was nice to meet another polyamorous couple. Their reply was a little shocked, 'We aren't polyamorous. We just like to play with other people.' So, we asked them what that meant. To them, because they weren't putting energy into developing other loving, romantic relationships, they weren't polyamorous. In their words, they were romantically monogamous that did kinky play with others. That opened our eyes a bit. So many ways of living in relationships.

That was then, this is now. We've been part of the Leather community for 20 years at this point, and I can say, from what I've seen, there is a difference in the Leather community and the Polyamory community. Different labels, different types of groupings. For example, we know more than one household that is a group of male Leather pups. In these groups, there is power exchange involved (which is talked about elsewhere in the book). The 'pups' usually have one 'Handler' that they answer to and most of the pups are in peer relationships unless they've ranked themselves as 'Alpha', 'Beta', etc. It's a fascinating way of creating a fun, playful, loving relationship that works for them. BTW.... pups aren't always male, but I don't see many female pups....at the moment anyway. I'm sure that will change over time.

There are also 'Leather Families' and 'Leather Tribes', 'Leather Houses'. Some of them consider themselves Polyamorous families, some do not. Sometimes it's borderline, or they just don't label themselves one way or the other – like many of us.

Each community has their own differences, but there are a lot of similarities in the Leather community with other communities, as well. If you attend a Leather event and just look for the polyamory aspects, you'll see some polyamory, some monogamy. You'll also see some solo poly individuals, but not as many as some other communities.

There are still some monogamous people in this community, so don't assume everyone is polyamorous. There is even a couple in Ohio that has created a 'Monogamous Pride' flag. This community has embraced multiple relationships easily, but the monogamous persons don't want it assumed that they are open to more relationships or play partners. So, they built their own symbol to express who they are.

That seems to be a common theme in the Leather world; creating pride flags for all the different groups. 'Monogamy, 'Leather', 'Polyamory, 'Pups', 'Bootblacks', 'D/s', 'Bears', 'Asexual', etc. If you attend a Leather event, you will see lots of people wearing vests, and on these vests are Backpatches of whatever 'House', 'Tribe', 'Group', or 'Club' they belong to, and various other patches and pins. Some of these flags are represented on these vests.

And the vests are just one of the differences you'll experience in the Leather community. It has its own culture. Regardless if you are poly or mono, that's just a small piece to this unique community. If you walk into a Leather event with no background or explanation of what to expect, it could be a little confusing. Just treat everyone with respect and if you'll do fine and over time will pick up on the differences.

Dan says...

In the Leather community, they have a variety of contests. Some are 'stand and model' (kind of a beauty contest for hot leather clad folk), and some are skill or teaching based. At the international level, there has been more than one poly pod that has won these contests. So, it is simply another 'accepted' style of relationships.

One aspect of Leather Culture I really enjoy is the openness and lack of judgment. People are still people, but I've never had anyone say to me 'You are doing Leather wrong'. Unfortunately, polyamory culture has a lot of opinions about the 'Right Way' to do things and if you are not doing it that way, you are doing it the Wrong Way. Leather is about finding you, your authentic you, no matter what that looks like – including being a vegan that never wears leather.

POLYAMORY AND
BUDDHISM

Dan says...

Tricycle, a leading American Buddhist magazine, has written about Buddhism and polyamory with reference to compersion. In Buddhism, the concept is known as mudita (and not limited to romantic relationships). Now, not to say that "Buddhist are Polyamorous", but some are, including me.

As a brief and simple view, Buddhist philosophy is full of great relationships tools; they start with know yourself and extend outward. One of the very first principles in Buddhism is that suffering is a result of attachments. Are we clinging to our relationships staying the same, to things not changing when new people show up, or wishing it was a different person your partner was interested in?

Another is to always approach your partners with loving kindness. This isn't to say that you must always do what they want or "roll over". But you can do what you need to do and still be compassionate to your partners.

Mindfulness, awareness of suffering caused by re-activity and habitual patterns, focus on self instead of an external cause being the "problem"...there is a lot Buddhism that can apply to relationships and making them healthy and loving.

Regarding sex in Buddhism, there is no list. There is no 'you can do this, but not that' (some specific traditions have developed a list, but they are cultural). Sexual misconduct is avoided. That is simply sex that causes harm, which normally is due to selfishness or dishonesty.

I'll also mention the Buddhist concept of the Four Immeasurables. What relationship would not benefit from Loving-kindness, vicarious joy (joy in other people's joy), compassion (both of others and oneself, and equanimity (keeping emotionally calm regardless of the situation).

Finally, I'll mention this. Dawn and I started practicing Polyamory nearly twenty years ago. About fifteen years ago, I started practicing Buddhism as well, and at the point, as this book is to be published, I am a novice Zen monk. My teacher is not only aware of polyamory but is actively polyamorous himself. There is no conflict. Love is a goodness.

POLYAMORY AND PAGANISM

Dawn says...

Another community where I learned a lot about Polyamory is the Pagan Community. You may have noticed that when Dan and I got together and decided to create our fantasy relationship, we jumped into a lot of different communities: Leather, Kink, Power Exchange, were a few of these, but another one was the Pagan Community. I had just found my calling as a Pagan and I wanted to learn as much as possible.

We attended events and festivals and wow, open relationships and 'festival' relationships were all around us. There is this bumper sticker that I used to have, that really described the environment we were in, 'All Acts of Love and Pleasure are Her Rituals', and this was embraced to the nth degree. Love. Sex. Pleasure. Embracing the God/Goddess as vessels, multiple loving partners. Making love under the stars or risking sunburn during the day in the fields of bonfires. These were some amazing experiences and it was through these events that I found my path of being a Qadishtu Priestess.

I spent my time with free spirits and hippies and nudists. It was amazing and really fed my spirit. The belief that multiple loving, sexual relationships is possible, is what spoke to my soul.

It's time for me to get back to festivals, especially the outdoor ones.

SACRED SPACES

Dan says...

Dawn requested that only she and I share our bed. Karen asked that I not take anyone else to the bed and breakfast where we had our commitment ceremony.

I used to think about these 'can this be just for you and me?' as kind of "anti-poly". I know some people who would suggest excluding places are just more rules, and that rules are just ways to give an illusion of safety to people who are scared.

I had to step back and realize that request like this - let's make this place or thing just "ours" - are not all the same. When Dawn first found out that I was taking Karen to Las Vegas, her first response was 'But that is where we got married!', and that is true. But we talked about that and decided that me and Karen visiting Las Vegas would not make it any less special that we got married there; it would not wipe away those good memories, and we would not experience it the same (note our tool 'Experience it Differently', which appears elsewhere in this book). But where Dawn decided that there wasn't really a good reason that I should avoid taking another loved one to some place special to us (the city of Las Vegas), she did ask that I not take Karen to the chapel where she and I got married. I could have debated that as well, suggested that it would still be special to me, etc., but, why? I had no interest or intention in taking Karen there regardless, and if it would make Dawn feel better, why not just be generous and agree? So, I did, and we were both happy with that (and Karen could not care less - there are plenty of wedding churches in Las Vegas if we wanted to visit one).

What is a reasonable request and what isn't? I can't decide for anyone else. Over time we have come to have a pretty balanced view between what should be held special by parts of a poly partners (like a specific bed) and what is just a panic or 'fear of not being special' request (avoid cities, stadiums, highways). And often it is temporary - maybe we will keep a new restaurant just us for a few days or weeks before we realize we would enjoy sharing it with our partners. And in truth, I have had lunch with one partner at a new place and for dinner brought another partner to the same place because I wanted to share a great find.

If you are having challenges with this one, and the request isn't one that causes logistical issues (like a request not to share a car), sometimes I've found patience is the solution. When Dawn asked me not to bring any new partners to the house, we already had another option, so I said 'Sure, but let's revisit this in a month'. And before that month was over, Dawn said 'well, actually, it is dumb to pay for a hotel room since we have all these extra rooms here...' And in some cases – don't share our bed – Dawn had a good reason for that and we are fortunate to have spare beds. So, after 18 years, we still don't share that bed. And although some in poly circles would suggest that such rules are the sign of a broken relationship, to us everything feels like it is working just fine.

Dawn says...

I'm fine with partners having special places with their partners. Well, I am now. At this point, with the partners I have, these special places are few and far between. Dan has a special place with Karen, and a special place with me. The boyfriend and I don't have a special place, but it could happen. He may have a special place with his wife, and if I asked him to take me there, he may say 'no, that's my place with my wife.' OK, there are literally thousands of other places we could go.

Though, I will admit that I tried to keep Las Vegas for Dan and me. I mean, that's where we got married. He and Karen wanted to go to a concert there. My response was, "not Las Vegas, that's our spot." His reply? "The whole damn town?". Ok. When you look at it, it does seem a little ridiculous. I asked him to give me a day or so to line up my emotions with the logic. He did so and then once I got it lined up, I was ok.

Above in his writing, Dan mentioned our bed. That's an odd thing that some people may resonate with and some may not. Remember that survivor stuff and past baggage stuff I mentioned in other places in the book? Well, most of that past baggage comes from me not being safe in my own bed, in my own house. For me to be able to sleep without nightmares and flashbacks, I need a safe space to sleep. If someone else's smell is in my bed or I feel someone else's energy in it, or I don't think it's 'my' safe space for some reason, I won't be able to sleep. And being poly, there are nights where I'm sleeping alone. My space must feel as safe as possible.

Dan can sleep with me in that bed because he's helped me build this safe spot. But, no one else does. I'd probably be ok if one of my partners slept with me in my bed, but that doesn't feel fair to Dan and his partners. So, sleeping with partners happens in the guest bedroom.

For most limits that I ask for in my relationships, I usually let them go at some point after doing some work or re-framing my emotions. But, this (the bed) is one of those things that may not change. With this one, my partners need to be ok with my limitation. This has nothing to do with a fear based on polyamory. It's my sacred sleeping space.

THRIVING AS AN ABUSE SURVIVOR

Dawn says...

I am an abuse 'survivor'. Actually, I'm glad to say, I'm a 'thriver', despite the abuse in my past.

There was a time that I couldn't use those words. There was a time that abuse 'victim' was the only way I could describe myself. Because of my past, I thought there wasn't any hope of finding love, simply because I couldn't trust people enough to allow them to get close to me.

One day the Universe was tired of how I was treating myself and smacked me upside the head (though that's another story for another book; if you ever want to know more about it, feel free to ask me).

From that point on, I started the hard work of my healing path. This meant getting past my fears, getting past my self-hate, getting past the memories, getting past the shame of what happened. During this time, mine and Dan's friendship turned into something more, and we started creating a fantasy life. It was hard. There was a lot of hard work involved to jump these hurdles (and sometimes smash through them) that were in place for my protection: defense mechanisms that were beneficial as a child but not so much now. It was such a struggle, but it was through that struggle that some of these tools were born that we share with you now.

When you come with past baggage that gets in the way of relating with people, it can be difficult for everyone involved, not only me and my partner, but any partner that he brought into the mix and any partner that I brought into the mix, and their partners. It's a ripple effect that takes patience and understanding by the partners, and hard work by the person with the baggage.

I went through a lot of moments of jealousy, a lot of moments of being triggered, a lot of moments in that 'flight or fight' mode that feels so crappy and confusing. I was lucky that the work I was doing with various counselors and therapists was helping me build the foundation with my partners to help us through those moments. And I kept doing the work that can be so amazingly difficult as I worked to change my habitual patterns of reaction and how I interacted with the world and all these feelings that arose.

You see, my main defense mechanism was to numb myself from heavy emotions and keep myself out of 'un-safe' situations. Well, polyamory is going to change all of that. I'm now feeling, because ...well .... love. But, once I opened to that emotion, I can't make the decision to only feel love. All the other emotions come with it; jealousy, anger, sadness, loneliness, unworthiness; all that stuff that I had crammed down to survive now jets to the surface. And if I want to continue feeling love, I must deal with all the other stuff as well. So, I did, and do.

At the beginning it was super hard. Ugh. Emotions. There were many times I just wanted to curl in my numb bubble again. But I took the leap of faith that if I had found one person to love, Dan, I could allow myself to love others like I really wanted to do.

That meant more work. Luckily, I ended up with a couple of amazing therapists at the beginning. And the work has paid off. Not that I'm completely done with it, even after 20 years. But, it's so much easier now (knock on wood). I recognize when I'm getting out of whack and control it a lot easier. I'm MUCH more open with people.

I mean....

My life is amazing right now. It's stressful because of the business venture we are involved in, but all in all I'm happy.

I'm at the point where I believe the men and women in my life have been brought to me for a reason. Though I've already learned this with Dan, I'm now experiencing it with Raymond and the girlfriend and the occasional friend/play partner: not all men are like my abusers from a long time ago. I can trust people. People can be trustworthy. I may not have learned this if I hadn't followed the path of polyamory.

It struck me last night when Raymond called just to hear my voice, and when chatting with the new guy friend through messenger. All these guys in my life are very different than the men that I grew up around.

As of the writing of this book, I have a couple of partners. Each of them has their own views on the world and don't feel the need to convince anyone else with a different path that their path is right/wrong. They are all about learning new things and being their authentic selves in an ethical manner. This seems to be a theme in polyamory. Neither of them are into emotional blackmail or passive aggressive behavior. This seems to be a theme in healthy relationships. I'm able to have my walls down around them, and not have to worry about getting hurt. And if my feelings are hurt, it's not through any intention of theirs.

A happy, loving life is possible after many, many years of abuse. As a 'survivor/thriver' work is needed, which is why we are sharing the tools we've learned. But it is possible to work through all the baggage.

There is a fullness to this feeling that I can't describe. I can love and be loved. I never thought this much love would be possible in my life.

Dan says...

When we began looking into polyamory as a lifestyle choice, we wanted to be certain that this could truly be a healthy choice. Some told us that polyamory was only chosen by those who were raised with some deficiency. Those that can't commit to relationships, or are too promiscuous to handle monogamy, or just haven't 'grown up' yet. So, we did our research. In short, what we found (and I hope if you have any doubts, you'll see for yourself) that polyamorous people are a mixed bag. Some are abuse survivors. Some have had crappy relationships. Some have mental health challenges. Some suffer from sleep disorders, depression, and physical challenges. And - some do not. As a matter of fact, we found that there were no patterns, no 'aha' moments that lead us to figure out what brought people to polyamory. Some are liberal hippy types; some are hard core Republicans; some are Christians, and some are skeptics. And everything else in between.

I guess the long-winded point I am trying to get here is, we have not found any social or background indicator on why people are polyamorous. And the real point behind that - you are poly because you are. Not because you are lacking, or wounded, or deficient. Some people are poly, some are not.

TRANSITIONING FROM A NON-POLYAMOROUS COUPLE

Dan says...

When Dawn and I started dating, it was with the idea that we would still see other people. We didn't know what that would look like, and we wanted each other to be part of our life, but we also recognized that the normal model of 'two people and never a glance elsewhere' wasn't going to be who we were. We didn't have the language for it at the time; just that our relationship would include other people in some fashion.

At first, we tried swinging. We would go to a club, find other people to have sex with, have sex, go home. Should have been pretty great but wasn't really fulfilling. Next, we tried the kink scene, whips and chains and spankings and power exchange; and this was a lot more fun for us - both the community and the scene around it - but was only part of what we were looking for.

It wasn't until later we heard the term polyamory and had that 'aha!' moment.

Many couples that are involved in polyamory nowadays don't start with the idea that they will ever be anything other than a couple. They decide to pursue polyamory after some time - we know friends who were monogamous for months, others for decades. The 'why' varies and often starts with a different path (such as us with swinging and kink).

An important note here: we have a section about that "Why" elsewhere in the book and it is a really important part of the picture. This section assumes you have looked at the Why and are ready to get going.

Plus, we have another section of the book on how to find people. Both of those sections are great for anyone getting involved in polyamory. Those two, added to this one, complete the picture for an existing couple moving into polyamory.

Ok! So, enough prequel, let's do it, the first step is to (if you can and match up in such a way that it works) have sex. Yes, seriously. And then get a good night's rest. Then the next morning have a nice breakfast, grab some paper and pencils, and start noodling some stuff down. Why sex first? Because we want to avoid speaking from a place of lust. Now, lust might be part of why you are exploring polyamory, the desire for more and different sex, and that is a great reason. Polyamory isn't all about sex – that is swinging – but it is, for many people, a fun part of it. But you want to have a clear and balanced head and heart going into this conversation, and sex is both a great way to connect to someone as well as...well, clear the pipes.

So, we are sitting down and ready to start. Dedicate a few hours to this conversation. The paper and pens are to jot down thoughts and ideas – you are not writing rules or agreements, just ideas or things you might want to talk about later. And now, just talk. Be open and see if you can let things flow. This might be a fun adventure for some; for others, this is a scary and almost heartbreaking moment of vulnerability. Normally, moving into polyamory as a couple isn't about a lack of love, but if you are worried it might be, ask. Do you still love me? Do you want me? These questions, if they are hiding in your head somewhere, need to be brought to the table. Give them a voice. Don't make accusations, but just request for information. And if the answer is "I don't know" then that is ok too. Let each other talk. Use your paper to make notes of things to come back to later; but let each other finish each sentence before you throw out a "but but but".

If things get emotionally charged – and they probably will, one way or another – that is ok. Be ok with taking breaks – either of you should be able to say, "let's take 5" and go for a walk around. Breathe and come back to the table and remember you are a team, working on something together.

Here are some specifics you might want to discuss. And at this point, you might decide to record them in some way. I am a fan personally of having written agreements as it helps to really lock in what you expect from each other. Assumptions and surprises make things harder to navigate; writing things down can help. But with this caveat – what you write down today might not be how things are tomorrow. Think of it as a starting point.

- Will you date as a couple or as individuals? Dating as a couple has its own set of challenges – other spots in this book you'll see references to both unicorn hunting and coamory.
- Are there physical locations you don't want to share? Meaning, are there places that are off limits of bringing a partner too? The bed at home, or the house in general, or the restaurant where she proposed to you, or work or church? There are lots of reasons to want to avoid having new people at - if you are not out at work and you take multiple partners to the company Christmas party, it might cause a stir. Be

careful you don't get too restrictive though - when we had a 'no dates at the house' agreement, we didn't think about how much in hotel rooms we would have to pay for!

- Courtesy request. Here is where we list items that are simple 'makes my life easier' preferences. Now, we are not saying you should avoid all the things that are uncomfortable, nor are we saying that just because it is uncomfortable it is wrong (see section on uncomfortable vs wrong). But for us, we have some small things we listed here that we view as simply a nice to have (or not have) as part of this. Ours include 'take a shower before you come home from a date', 'change your shirt if your partner wears heavy cologne/perfume', 'let me know before you get home if you have new hickies'. These are not rules, they are simply treating each other with a small kindness.

- Safer sex. This one should be written down in detail. I don't want to tell you the number of times we have heard people share they said one thing but heard something else ('when she said always wear condoms, I didn't realize it meant oral as well).

- Communication plan. Can I text you while you are on a date? Can I expect an immediate reply? Do you care if I call if I can't find the can opener? Or do these feel like you are intruding on my partner time?

- Communication plan part 2. Are the questions 'when do you leave, get home, and where are you going?' too restrictive? Do they feel controlling? Or do they just feel like common communication because someone must be home to let the dog out.

And here is your start. The rest of the book is full of tools and ideas and even some 'don't do what we did' examples. But take a moment to smile at each other and let the adventure begin.

Dawn says...

And we really did take small steps to begin with. We did some toe-dipping instead of jumping off the deep end. We knew that we wanted to have a relationship where loving and/or having sex with others was part of the plan and expectations, but we didn't know how we were going to react to seeing/knowing our other partner was with someone else.

There wasn't a way to know how we'd react if one of our partners fell in love with someone, until it happened, but we could do some testing to see if we got jealous in regard to our partners having sex with others. That's where the swing clubs came into play. Since they are usually about sex, then it wasn't going to hurt someone's feelings if I had sex with them and didn't come back. So, we did that a couple of times.

We talked about it the next day. We started out as a couple and would meet other couples. Then, we'd swap and have sex with each other's partners in the same room, then separate rooms. All that seemed to go well.

We dated women together in a coamory dynamic. That went pretty well.... somewhat.... well ok, not really. Out of the women we dated, there was only one that really liked dating us together. I've probably mentioned this elsewhere in the book, but she loved the energy that Dan and I had together and had no interest in dating us separately. That worked out for a while, but it ended up that she needed more time from us and with our jobs, kids, and projects, we just couldn't squeeze enough time out of our calendar. So, she moved on to the next couple that had more time available.

We tried again, but Dan and I are just too different for coamory to really work for us. So, we started dating separately. We had some agreements in place while we started wading into new waters. We dealt with things as they came up.

We had some agreements in place on how we'd communicate with each other during dates. These agreements changed over time as new experiences were introduced. Some agreements were added after discussion on whether they were necessary, some agreements dropped off after we outgrew them.

It's funny, but we still change clothes before coming home if we've been cuddling with another partner. Or before our nesting partner comes home if we had our date at the house. And we still shower after having sex with one partner and meeting up with another. Neither one of us feels we are limiting the other and we both want this agreement. It has to do with smell, not trying to limit a partner or to shame a partner. As a matter of fact, the way Dan asks me if I've had sex with a partner is to ask me if I had to take a shower. It's kind of cute actually.

So, over the last 20 years, we've gone from being in separate monogamous relationships, to dating each other, to getting married to each other with the intent of having an open relationship of some sort, to trying swinging, to trying coamory, to living polyamory. Each of us now have a couple of long-term partners and we've shared a house with one of Dan's partners.

We've stumbled along the way and fought to get over some hurdles, and there have been moments of flying high with some amazing experiences. Who knows what the future holds for each of us?

COUPLES PRIVILEGE

Dawn says...

So, as you may have noticed, Dan and I are in a polyamorous relationship that involves other partners. We are also a couple. We've raised kids together, pay bills together, run a business together and we share dreams and goals. Some may say we have 'couple's privilege', which is a descriptor that is usually used in a negative way.

But you will find that many polyamorous people start out as couples and then realize that they are different than other people and try this polyamory thing. As they do, there will be hurdles to jump; some will have to work around babysitting. Some will have to work around finances and figure out how dates and gifts get paid for. Many won't be willing to give away the kids, separate finances or divorce, just so they aren't a couple anymore. Which means those things must be thought about and worked through. It is what it is.

Raymond is married. I knew this when we started our relationship and felt it would be rude to ask for time that he was already spending with family. His kids and family come first. I respected him for this and felt it would be selfish to demand that he spend more time with me instead of his kids. Over time as his kids have gotten older, he's had more time available which we make use of, but I still have no interest in challenging him for equal time or 'if he really loved me, he'd spend more time with me.'

Just like, his wife keeps in touch with him while he and I are out. I also keep in touch with Dan. The boyfriend and I understand that we each have other partners and the way we do poly means we don't try to separate ourselves from our other partners. Now his wife, and my husband don't text us constantly, but if Dan needs to know where something is, he texts me. If the boyfriend's wife just got a picture of their new grandbaby, she sends it to him. It's not a big deal. Is it Couples privilege, or just the way the relationships are? I don't know how to label it or bother with a label at all. I do know that I come into any new relationship with responsibilities from my current relationships.

Polyamory doesn't happen in a vacuum. It's a mishmash of different relationships for most of us, and a couple of my partners happen to be coupled with others. Sometimes, if I want to go out with the girlfriend, she must discuss it with her husband. It's not asking permission necessarily but discussed to make sure someone can be home to walk the dog, who gets the car, who is picking up who after the date.

I'm not attached to what people want to call this. To me it's just a relationship style that is part of my poly pod, and I'll work with it as needed. As I said, I have no interest in challenging other relationship styles to make mine seem more valid or as valid.

Dan says...

For me, it is about balance and ethical treatment of each other. When I meet a new partner, they understand I have a life already in progress and that is part of who they are dating. That doesn't mean that if Dawn is uncomfortable, then they (the new partner) is 'second fiddle' or that by default Dawn gets 'her way'. But it does mean that if an existing responsibility intrudes on our time together, then I will do my best to compensate. In both directions. But I'll freely admit that I've got over 35 years of history with Dawn (yes, we've known each other for that long, although not in a relationship, but that is another story!). Does that equate to her having some privilege over a new partner? I suppose that depends on how you view the word. Perhaps it is relationship equity, perhaps it is a long-term bond, perhaps it is a privilege. But it does not prevent me from having ethical, loving, multi-partner relationships. It is simply different than if I was solo poly or some other love styles.

ONE PENIS POLICY

Dan says...

Sometimes you hear about a male/female couple exploring polyamory but with the requirement that polyamory is ok as long as only other women are part of it. So, he can have a girlfriend...and so can she. But her having a boyfriend/male lover is out of the question. This is often called the "one penis policy". In this style of polyamory, if the woman isn't bi, well, she is out of luck. As you might guess, it is the male partner that normally requires this rule.

The reason that a male would suggest (or simply impose) the 'one penis policy' may appear to be complex and varied, but once we cut through to the heart of it, it likely comes down to him feeling insecure and worried that he will lose his partner if she has more than one cock in her life. I totally understand that thinking - it is what I, and many other American males, had expressed to us by our peers growing up. And as adults, it is what the media shoved down our throats. It can be hard to get past those image makers.

And it should come as no surprise that most of the poly message boards I am on take a dim look at this poly - it is greeted with terms such as sexist, controlling, toxic, homophobic, and more. Whether you agree with those views or not, I'd suggest that the 'one penis policy' is not really a good rule for most relationships. I'll explain why.

I clearly recall the first time my girlfriend started being romantic with another male and it scared the crap out of me. It wasn't rational, and it wasn't that I wanted to control her - it was simply a deep fear that I was going to lose her. I was very fortunate that she acted like my partner and instead of giving me shit, she helped me get a grip on my heart and our security. She did not accept the 'one penis policy' and she let me know it - but she also held my hand and gave me time to get past the old tapes I was raised with. In truth, I wanted nothing but happiness and joy for her. It took time to develop the self-confidence to let go of what I was brought up with and decide for myself how I would feel.

Dawn says...

I do agree with Dan that if this is a 'policy' or 'agreement' set by one of the partners, it can be unhealthy. On the other hand, if both partners truly agree to this, it's just another form of mono-poly. I know a couple of poly pods that are one guy and a couple or more girls and they are totally happy in that configuration. And at least one of the poly pods I know, have been together for many years. The girls have no interest in dating other guys and when asked if they are upset about what appears to be a 'one penis policy', they are confused. This is what they wanted and what they looked for in a relationship.

So, if you are on the outside looking in, just remember that what you see could be a healthy relationship. It's not up to us to judge what is healthy and what isn't. Just because something doesn't work for you or even make sense to you, doesn't mean it doesn't work for someone else.

The issue is when you yourself are in a relationship that is limiting to one of the partners and that limited partner isn't happy with the limitation. That's when you'll have to look at it and see if it's something that will change through personal growth on the part of the person setting the limit, or if it's a deal breaker for you and time to find a relationship/s that will fulfill you.

NOT STRUGGLING WITH
A NEW PARTNER

Dan says...

Karen is normally a fairly slow mover in relationships. So when she met her new partner and they went from first date, then to 'love you', then to sleeping together, and then to weekends away in the span of just a few weeks (or so it felt like to me), I had a tough time with it because there didn't feel like there was time to either mentally or emotionally adjust. This can actually be very common when NRE (new relationship energy) hits.

So even when I am feeling confident and balanced and greet our partner's news that they have a new partner with enthusiasm and joy, the pace of that new relationship can be a challenge. In the case that I am describing here, it felt like being hit by the NRE train!

For me, the first thing I need to do is write out what my partner is doing, each aspect on its own line. This is to satisfy the thinking/logic part of my brain. In the above example, the lines would be:

- She met someone new
- They are having sex
- They are going off for a weekend away
- She loves him

Now, I look at each item mentally and ask myself "Is what she is doing ethical, within the agreements of our relationship, and is she openly communicating about it?". Although my emotional self might have some harsh criticism, I bring myself back to just the question with no attachment. Is it so or not? Does the fact that she loves him within what we, as polyamory people, can do without our agreements? If so, then a checkmark and move on to the next.

This checklist got me through that she wasn't doing anything "wrong". But I was still struggling with it emotionally, and that is ok. It meant I needed to look at my struggle.

I have found it very helpful to look at emotional turmoil like this as if it was a raging river. If you struggle against a river, you will get overwhelmed. Instead, let go. That is scary but allows you to focus on you. Flow with the situation as you can, breathe, and trust. Trust the river to carry you. Trust her to not forget you. NRE is powerful stuff. So, I tell her, I am struggling with the pace and will say something like "I will trust you not to lose me. I might need more reassurance. Can you set some time aside for me? Give me a few breaths to adjust to new things". I try not to resist the new relationship; instead, to remember to make sure I ask for help from my partner.

Dawn says...

When one of your partners starts dating a new person, it can be really challenging, and the challenges can be different from partner to partner and new person to new person. When Dan starts dating someone new, I immediately try to place them in a box and label them. This is because he dates and starts relationships for different reasons. Some are time limited on purpose by both parties, some are just generic dating for play, some are with an intent of forming a long-term relationship or at least have that potential. So, my brain tries to figure out who is who so that I can figure out how they fit into my partner's life and my life, if at all.

Thankfully, Dan started telling me 'I don't know' when I would ask how the new person fits in. Raymond learned this trick as well. You wouldn't think that would work, but it kept me from being able to label them or put them into a structured box. It helped with my struggle with a new partner. Instead, I could have an open mind and just allow whatever was going to happen to happen. That's where the mantra of 'waiting is' would come in handy. This is the idea that we don't know what is going to happen, so wait and find out. All will be revealed in due time.

At that point, all I ask is that I'm kept in the loop of whatever is going on and whatever might be in the future. Management of surprises and not keeping secrets helps me feel much more stable in whatever relationship I'm in, especially after the experience with the past boyfriend.

THE GOOD STUFF

Dan says...

One thing that Dawn and I noticed as we wrote this book was, we didn't share a lot of the good stuff about polyamory. Granted, this is intended to be a book of tools to deal with the challenging aspects of polyamory and not a 'look how great it is' review, but in truth, it is really great.

I have come to believe that life really is much shorter than we realize. So, although perhaps there is an afterlife or some form of rebirth, I instead think it is best to assume this is the one and only ride. So, live it. Be as big and authentic and you as you can be. Find out what is important to you and make sure you make it part of your life.

Moreover, although sometimes polyamory hurts – from the struggle of finding someone, to the realization that a person you deeply love will not be part of your life anymore, and everything in the middle - the benefits and positives are without compare. Nothing in my heart needs to be ignored. No desire needs to be forgotten. If I want (as sometimes I do) to interact and love a new person who has a different perspective on the world, ok, I do. If I want to practice celibacy and keeping things very minimal and quiet and self-absorbed (as I sometimes do), then so be it. However, I usually am in the middle of that – and if I catch the eye of a person and they smile back, then I am allowed to let it flow as it will. Or not. And it is ok.

Love can't be undervalued or understated. In our days toward the end, when we are tired and ready to relax and reflect on our walk on this globe, it would be a shame to look back on opportunities missed. Yet I will – I have been motivated by fear or laziness on occasion and made poor decisions. However, I have made skillful and courageous ones. I've also made some dumb ones that I can laugh at, and lots and lots of silly things that give me a smile. However, it is the love I've shared that makes it worthwhile. Love as the root of compassion, sharing, caring, intimacy. What a gift I've been given to find polyamory and find like-minded folks. Sometimes I feel like I have the ultimate life hack – "Does love make you happy? This simple trick gets you as much as you can handle!". Alas, the truth shared in the poly circles still applies: Love is infinite, time is not. Our time is not unlimited. Don't wait to create an open and willing you. Love finds a way; you have to open the door.

Dawn says...

After writing this book and re-reading it before sending it to the editor, we were concerned that people would blow off polyamory as a relationship choice because of all the work that is involved. I just wanted to mention that this is a book of tools, and tools are created or gathered because something needs to be fixed.

Therefore, we shared a lot about the sucky times we had over the last almost 2 decades.

But, don't read this book and be fooled into thinking that polyamory is all about 'fixing things' and needing tools. We've had many, many fantastic moments along the way. I certainly wouldn't be putting all this effort into maintaining multiple loving relationships if I weren't also having a good time and experiencing joy like I haven't experienced before.

For us, this is a fantasy life that we've turned into reality. All those times in the past where I met someone and had tingles but couldn't follow through with them because I was in a monogamous relationship, I can now follow through with. I can interact with people on the most intimate level and I don't have to give up my current relationships in the process. I can allow the love to flow instead of damming it and living with resentment or guilt. The world is an open oyster with unique pearls to be discovered.

There are so many beautiful souls out there and I can love them and be in love with them. Just as I currently love and am in love with some amazing people. As Dan said, we just have to be open to it. Love big. Love courageously. Love deep. Love often. Love without regret.

More Dan & Dawn

Dan and Dawn have presented at over 100 events around North America. They are the authors of multiple books and the popular Kink Starter Cards.

They are also the co-hosts of the Erotic Awakening internet radio show, an educational podcast that explores "all things erotic"; co-directors of the Columbus Space, an alternative community centre; and mentioned in several books, articles, and other media.

"They move between clear and simple presentation of facts and information to personal stories of their fascinating experiences together, energizing their audiences with the ease and grace of people that enjoy what they are doing"

Thay Dan (pronounced "tie") is also an ordained novice monk in a Zen tradition.

Dawn is also a Qadishtu (pronounced kadishtu) priestess and is ordained and licensed clergy in the state of Ohio.

Awards & Nominations and Community Service Positions Include:
- Member's Choice Presenter of the Year Award 2016
- Great Lakes Title 2010
- PRSCO 2010 Presenter of the Year Award

erotic
awakening

Keep up with Dan & Dawn via the Erotic Awakening Podcast
http://www.eroticawakening.com/podcast/

Made in the USA
Las Vegas, NV
08 June 2021